GHOSTS OF PIRACY PAST

Cable Theft Investigations

Darno Von DeJohnette

DeJohnette Publishing Group

Copyright © 2020 Darno Von DeJohnette

All rights reserved

The characters and events portrayed in this book are fictitious. Any similarity to real persons, living or dead, is coincidental and not intended by the author.

No part of this book may be reproduced, or stored in a retrieval system, or transmitted in any form or by any means, electronic, mechanical, photocopying, recording, or otherwise, without express written permission of the publisher.

ISBN: 9798584572822
ASIN : B08R6RWTDL

Cover design by: Art Painter
Library of Congress Control Number: 2018675309
Printed in the United States of America

Dedication:

To the private security investigators who tirelessly resolve cable television theft of service cases, your dedication and expertise shine a light on integrity and justice. Your unwavering commitment protects vital resources and ensures fairness for all. Thank you for your vigilance and hard work in safeguarding our communities.

So you've decided to steal cable. Myth: Cable piracy is wrong. Fact: Cable companies are big faceless corporations, which makes it okay.

HOMER SIMPSON

CONTENTS

Title Page
Copyright
Dedication
Epigraph
Prologue
CHAPTER ONE ... 1
CHAPTER TWO ... 27
CHAPTER THREE ... 60
CHAPTER FOUR ... 93
CHAPTER FIVE ... 111
CHAPTER SIX ... 126
CHAPTER SEVEN ... 143
CHAPTER EIGHT ... 156
CHAPTER NINE ... 171
CHAPTER TEN ... 180
Epilogue ... 203
Books By This Author ... 209
Acknowledgement ... 213
About The Author ... 215

PROLOGUE

Michael Devon Smith grew up in Chicago on the city's West Side. He had an above average IQ, but he never let it go to his head. His associates often referred to him as the neighborhood 'egg head.' But what they didn't know was that Smith was born with a 'gift' which made him special. Throughout his life that gift protected him, shielding him from the many bad decisions he made along the way.

But leaving Chicago was not one of them. After spending a few years resting and recuperating in the country, he moved to the west coast.

With the expansion of cable television services in the 1990s, the public's hunger for video entertainment grew proportionately. Cable piracy (a.k.a., theft of services) became rampant, resulting in millions of dollars in lost revenue. The overwhelming criminal activity forced cable companies to hire specially trained investigators to mitigate losses by actively pursuing the arrest and prosecution of cable pirates.

It was more than intuition that led Smith to Metro Cablevision. On a mild December day while walking to his job, he saw a young, attractive woman. The 'voice' in his head told him to speak with her. Smith ignored the message, and kept walking. The voice became more assertive and demanding, instructing him to seize the opportunity and speak with the young woman. Smith eventually gathered the courage, and decided to speak with her. What she told him set him on the path that changed his life.

But his path was not an easy one. Enduring personal hardships, and the pressures of a hostile work environment, he eventually succeeded in securing a position in the security department. There he became Metro Cablevision's first cybercrime investigator.

CHAPTER ONE
Suspect Contact

Arresting people for stealing cable television services was just part of the job. He pushed the report aside, lifted his eyes and glanced down the street. The target's white SUV was parked in the driveway. Someone was home. Pulling the cell phone from its cradle, he proceeded to dial the non-emergency number to the local police department. A dispatcher's voice answered.

"Dispatcher 21, how can I help you?"

"Hi. My name is Michael Smith. I am an investigator for Metro Cablevision. The reason for this call is that I am in the process of contacting a person suspected of illegally intercepting our cable television services. And I would like to have an officer respond, standby and preserve the peace while I conduct the investigation."

"Okay Michael. Are you at the location now?"

"I'm parked about a half block away, and I can see the residence from here."

"Are you in a marked Cablevision truck?"

"No. I'm in a red, unmarked Chevy Blazer."

"What is the address that you are going to?"

"We will be going to 5109 Via Torres."

"Are you armed?"

"No, I'm not."

"What is your cell phone number?"

"It's area code 619, 977-5555."

"Okay Michael, we'll have an officer meet you there as soon as possible. It might take a while. There are several calls pending, but someone will get to you as soon as they can."

"No problem. I appreciate your assistance. Thank you."

"You're welcome."

Smith settled back into the driver's seat as

he placed the cell phone into its cradle. He picked up his report, glanced down the street once more, and then began filling out the field investigation form.

"Time of arrival 1730 hours; called PD at 1745 hours."

Smith glanced up the street. The lights were on inside the residence. He looked at the clock on the dashboard. It was 5:49 PM, and daylight was beginning to fade. A slight chill hung in the autumn air. Smith settled back and waited.

Forty-five minutes passed before the black and white patrol car pulled up next to Smith's unmarked vehicle. He pressed the button and lowered the driver side window.

"Good evening officer. I'm Michael Smith with Metro Cablevision."

"What's going on?"

"A few weeks ago, we received a call from an anonymous tipster that the folks at 5109 Via Torres were receiving cable television services that they were not paying for. I came out on the 3rd of October and checked the cable line. I found that the line was connected illegally. I took several photographs, and then disconnected the cable wire from our equipment. I placed two red audit tags on the line and secured the pedestal with a special lock. Three days ago, I came back to re-inspect the connections. I found that the lock had been removed, and the cable wire was again illegally reconnected. My tags had been removed. Here are the photos."

"Okay, so what are we doing?"

"This is a misdemeanor under California Penal Code 593d. Normally what happens in a case like this is we do a knock and talk. If we get permission to enter and all the elements of the crime are present, I may do a 10-16, citizen's arrest for the violation. Depending upon the circumstances it could end up just being an admonishment. I won't know until we get inside."

"Okay, let us go. I'll follow you."

The patrol car pulled away, and did a 180, stopping just to the rear of Smith's vehicle.

"Okay," Smith whispered to himself. "It's show time."

He shifted his car into drive and pulled out

of the parking space. The two vehicles stopped a short distance from the suspect's residence. Smith got out and walking a few steps ahead of the police officer, stopped at the door and knocked four times. There was rustling inside. A moment later, the door opened. The resident looked bewildered at the sight of the two men standing at his front door.

"Can I help you?"

"Are you the primary resident here?" Smith asked.

"Yes I am. What is this all about?"

"Sir, my name is Michael Smith, and I am an investigator with Metro Cablevision. The reason that I am here, as you probably realize, is because of the cable television services you are receiving and are not paying for. I would like to come inside and talk to you about it."

Smith presented his photo identification.

"Sure, but the cable was on when we moved in."

"I understand, but just so you know, the officer is here as a precaution of safety and to preserve the peace while I conduct this investigation. The investigation is being conducted for Metro Cablevision."

Smith and the police officer entered the house and took a few steps beyond the threshold. The man closed the door behind them.

"Like I said, the cable was on when we moved in."

"And how long have you been living here?" Smith asked.

"A little over a year," he replied.

"Is there anyone else in the house beside you?"

"Just my wife and two kids; they're in the family room."

Smith looked around. The house was clean and tastefully decorated. The smell of scented candles gave the place a warm, cozy feeling. He observed that there was no television in this room. The clock on the wall displayed 6:37. Smith wrote the arrival and contact time into his log.

"You have a nice home, sir. May we look at

the television?"

"Sure, we were just about to eat dinner. We're in the family room."

"Is there a television in the family room that is connected to the cable television service?"

"Yes."

"How many televisions do you have in the house?"

"We have three all together; one in the family room; one in our bedroom; and one in the kid's room."

"Sir, do you have some form of ID; a driver's license?"

"Yes," he said, pulling the wallet from his back pocket. He removed the driver's license and handed it to Smith.

"Is there a problem?" he asked.

"Well, sort of," responded Smith cautiously. "The cable service being used here is not legally connected, and that's a violation of the California Penal Code. Is your full name John David Seltzer?"

"Yes. What kind of trouble are we talking about?"

Smith did not reply immediately. When he finished writing the suspect's information onto the field investigation form, he glanced up and smiled.

"We'll discuss that in a few minutes. Let us look at the television."

Seltzer led the investigators to the room, where his wife and children were watching Nickelodeon on a 32" Panasonic color television. Smith wrote a comment on his note pad, and then turned the page of his field investigation form.

"You say that you have lived here for a little over a year?"

"Yes. We moved here in September last year."

"And the cable service was on at that time?"

"Yes."

"Do you mind if I change the channels?"

"No, go right ahead."

"How are you doing this evening ma'am?" Smith politely acknowledged the woman and her children. "We won't be awfully long. I know you folks are just about to eat dinner, so I will wrap this up as quickly as possible. Just so you will know and to put your mind as ease, nothing is going to happen tonight, except maybe the issuance of a ticket. It is just a citation, that is all. No one's going to jail."

Smith smiled and glanced at the two little boys curled up on the couch. It was more for their benefit than Seltzer's wife. He did not want the kids to think for a moment that either of their parents would be going to jail. Mrs. Seltzer sighed, smiled as she nodded in acknowledgment, and then continued with her chores. Mr. Seltzer stood rigid, as Smith surfed through the channels.

"Okay, the television is receiving all of the cable channels," Smith said, as he returned to Nickelodeon. "I'm just going to take a picture of the TV now."

He removed a small digital camera from his pocket and snapped two quick pictures. He turned to Seltzer.

"May I see the other televisions?"

Seltzer did not reply, but simply began to walk in the direction of the master bedroom. Smith followed. The officer stayed behind in the family room, making small talk with the two boys.

The television in the master bedroom was also connected to the cable services. Smith verified each channel that it was receiving and jotted more notes onto his pad. He took photos of the television and the cable channel that it displayed.

There was a 13" TV in the kids' room, tuned to Cartoon Network. Smith jotted down some notes, and then proceeded to check the remaining channels. When he was done, he snapped two photographs of the television displaying the Cartoon Network logo.

"I see that all of your televisions are receiving the complete basic cable channel line-up," Smith announced. "And you say that the cable service was on when you moved in?"

"Yes, it was. I thought someone would eventually come out and disconnect it, but no one ever did."

"I see. So, the cable service never went off?"

"No. It's been on for the entire time."

"That's interesting, because I came out here a few weeks ago, found the line active and disconnected it."

Smith showed Seltzer photographs of the illegal cable connection.

"Here are the red audit tags that I attached to the line after I disconnected it. I also secured the equipment inside the pedestal with a special lock."

Seltzer looked at the photographs but said nothing. Smith turned the page of his report.

"Then, three days ago, I came out to re-inspect the line, and it was back on again. As you can see in these photographs, my audit tags have been removed. How do you explain that?"

"I can't."

"Hmmm, I see. So, you never noticed that the cable service had stopped working?

"No. I do not watch television that much.

I'm usually busy doing other things."

"I understand. Who do you think reconnected the cable service outside?"

"I don't know."

"Did you call anyone to connect the service for you?"

"No, I didn't have to. It's always worked."

"Did you call Metro Cablevision and have the service turned on?"

"No."

"Is anyone here a cable customer?"

"No."

"Does anyone here pay for cable service?"

"No."

"Have you ever had cable service at any other address?"

"Yes."

"Where was that?"

"It was at our old house."

"And was the cable service in your name?"

"It was either my name or my wife's name. I can't remember."

"But you did pay for cable service?"

"Yes."

"Did you have Metro Cablevision service?"

"Yes, I think it was."

"So, you know that you're supposed to pay for the cable service?"

"Yes."

"Well didn't you think it was strange that you were getting cable service without paying for it?"

"Well, I guess so. I thought someone would eventually come out and disconnect it. I guess I really didn't think much about it."

"So, you thought it was strange, but you didn't call Metro Cablevision to let us know that the service was on and that we should come out and disconnect it?"

"No," Seltzer responded, holding back a

chuckle.

"Did you ever call the company, and say, order the cable service?"

"No, I didn't have to. It was already on."

"Didn't you think it was wrong, and maybe even illegal to use the cable service without paying for it?"

"Frankly, I didn't give it very much thought."

Smith turned the page of his field investigation form. He studied the document for a moment, creating a buffer of silence, and giving himself time to contemplate the next set of responses.

"I'm going to give you a copy of California Penal Code 593d, and I'm going to read the section of the law that relates to this case."

Smith removed a page from his field investigation form and handed it to Seltzer. The print was small, almost too small to read in the restrained light.

"I realize that the print is small," Smith said abruptly, "so please bear with me as I read the relevant section."

Smith had his own copy of the Penal Code section; one with much larger print. He read the first two paragraphs, and then summarized the meaning in layman's terms.

"It means that anyone who uses the cable service without permission and without paying for it is guilty of a public offense. The violation is a misdemeanor and is prosecutable in California. Do you understand?"

"Yes, but I didn't hook it up."

"It doesn't matter if you connected the cable, or if you had someone else connect it for you. If you are maintaining the unauthorized connection, using the service without paying for it, you are guilty of a public offense."

Smith momentarily broke eye contact with Seltzer. He looked down at the field investigation form and turned the page.

"Now I am going to ask you a few questions that may seem a little odd, but I have to ask them. They are simple yes or no answers."

Seltzer did not respond. He was still looking over his copy of California Penal Code

593d, trying to determine what penalties he might be facing.

"Do you speak and understand English?"

"Yes."

"Do you understand that I am not a police officer?"

"Yes."

"Do you understand that I am not connected with the government in any way?"

"Yes."

"Do you understand that I am a private citizen employed by Metro Cablevision?"

"Yes."

"And do you understand that I am conducting this investigation for Metro Cablevision?"

"Yes."

"Is it your choice to cooperate with this investigation, to provide true and honest information?"

Seltzer took a deep breath, then calmly

stated, "Yes."

"Thus far, have you been honest and truthful during this investigation?"

Almost too quickly Seltzer responded, "Of course."

Smith hesitated a few seconds, allowing the silence to temporarily disarm his suspect. Having worked hundreds of cable theft cases, he could tell when someone was genuinely dishonest, or just trying to hide information. Smith continued the interview.

"Did you voluntarily grant us permission to enter your residence?"

This was an easy question that allowed Seltzer to feel comfortable and confident. He answered in a relaxed tone, "Yes."

Smith did not hesitate and went immediately to the next question.

"Did you give me permission to inspect the televisions, cable lines, equipment, etc.?"

"Yes."

Smith slowed his rhythm and spoke in a low monotone.

"Have any promises been made as to the outcome of this investigation?"

Seltzer seemed surprised at this question. His mind told him logically, that the next answer would be "yes"; but it was not. Scanning his memory, Seltzer answered slowly and deliberately.

"No, no promises have been made."

Smith allowed the answer to resonate for a moment, and then smoothly followed with another *no-brainer*.

"Are you the primary resident here?"

Seltzer seemed to listen more carefully to the questions before answering, "Yes."

"Is the cable service in your name?"

"No."

"Have you ever had cable service at any other address?"

"Yes, I think so. Yes."

"Having read the California Penal Code, would you agree that intercepting cable services, which you are not authorized to receive, is a crime?"

Seltzer diverted his eyes briefly, as he responded, "Yes."

"Just a few more questions and we will be finished," Smith assured him. "Have you ever seen any ads in newspapers, magazines or on television, or heard anything relating to cable theft as being a crime?"

"No, I haven't."

"Have you been completely honest during this interview?"

Smith locked eyes with Seltzer and did not blink. Almost gasping for his next breath, Seltzer responded, "Yes, I have."

Smith sighed and turned the page of the field investigation form.

"When I came to the door, I identified myself as an investigator for Metro Cablevision. I presented you with my photo identification and explained that I was here because we found the cable service had been illegally reconnected. Is that correct?"

"Yes."

"I also explained that the officer was present as a precaution of safety and to preserve the peace. And that using the cable service without authorization is a prosecutable offense. Is that correct?"

"Yes."

"When I complete my investigation, I am required as a matter of policy to write a case narrative. That narrative will be submitted to the District Attorney along with the officer's crime report. What the District Attorney does with the case, I cannot say. I have no authority or influence over the DA, and he may issue the case, or he may not. It is entirely up to him. If he finds there is substantial cause to prosecute the case, he may do so. He may also file additional charges. I cannot say what the DA will or will not do. Therefore, I cannot make any promises as to the outcome of this investigation. Do you understand?"

"Yes."

"When I came to the door, I asked for permission to enter. You voluntarily granted us permission to enter. I did not say that I had a search warrant or any other instrument that would allow me to enter your home without permission. Is that correct?"

"Yes."

Smith stepped forward, pushing the field investigation form toward Seltzer with one hand, and a pen in the other.

"Please sign here to show that these are your responses to the questions."

Seltzer took the pen and glanced over the form. He then scribbled his name onto the document. Smith turned the page.

"Please sign here to show that these are your answers to *these* questions."

Seltzer looked at the page of questions and reviewed his "yes" and "no" answers. He seemed satisfied with what he saw and signed the form again.

Smith turned to the next page and recited two more questions.

"Did the investigator provide you with a copy of California Penal Code 593d?"

"Yes."

"Did the investigator read the section of the law that's related to this case?"

"Yes."

"Please initial here."

Seltzer initialed the form and gave the pen back to Smith.

"Now there's just one more thing," Smith said, as he pulled the digital camera from his pocket. "I just need to take a photograph of you. If you would not mind, I would like for you to stand in front of the wall here; where there's a clear, white background."

Seltzer complied, and the camera flashed.

"Thank you, Mr. Seltzer. As I stated before, using the cable service that you are not authorized to receive is a prosecutable offense. I am now placing you under citizen's arrest for violation of California Penal Code 593d, sub "a", sub "1", knowingly and willfully maintaining an unauthorized cable television connection. The officer will now issue you a citation."

Smith took a step back, closed his notebook and handed Seltzer's driver's license to the officer. The officer pulled a citation book from his pocket and began to write the ticket. A few minutes later, he was finished.

"Okay Mr. Seltzer, you have been placed under citizen's arrest by the representative from the cable company for 593d, cable theft," the officer stated. "This is a misdemeanor. You are not going to jail today. Technically, you could, but you are just being cited and released. I will need your signature. Please sign here. This ticket is your promise to appear in court on the date and time indicated. You may receive a notice in the mail from the court, but in case you do not, remember that this is your court date. You must be there; otherwise, a warrant will be issued for your arrest. Do you have any questions?"

"No."

"Thank you, sir, and have a good day. This is your copy."

The two men walked out the door, and Seltzer closed it behind them. Smith walked to the patrol car with the officer.

"I'll need your information for the citizen's arrest form. Do you have a business card?"

"Yes, I do," responded Smith as he pulled a card from his notebook. "When do you need my report?"

"I'll need it as soon as possible. Tomorrow is my Friday. How soon can you get it to me?"

"I can go back to the shop and start pounding it out tonight. Or I can start on it first thing in the morning. Either way I should have it at your office no later than noon tomorrow. Is that okay?"

"That will be fine. You can leave it at the front desk. They'll put it in my box."

"There's just one more thing. I need your ID number."

"I'll give you a card as soon as I get a crime case number for you."

"Great. While you are doing that, I'm going to disconnect the cable wire."

Smith put on his tool belt and headed for the cable pedestal, while the officer contacted his dispatcher for a case number. Smith opened the little green box, and snipped the wire marked "09." He pulled a terminating filter lock from his tool pouch and attached it to the directional tap, securing it from future possible tampering. He put a fresh audit tag on the line, and then zip tied the line together in a loop. He took the digital camera from his pocket and took another photograph of the disconnected line. He then closed the pedestal and secured it with a special lock. Taking off his tool belt, he placed it into his vehicle and returned to the patrol car with his notebook.

The officer pulled a citizen's arrest form from the organizer in the trunk of his car and passed it to the investigator. Smith quickly printed his name, business address and phone number, date of birth and driver's license number. He signed the document and handed it back to the officer.

"This is your case number," he said. "My ID number is also on the card."

Smith took the card, looked at the case number written on the back, then jotted it down in his field investigation form along with the officer's name and ID number.

"Thanks Gary. I appreciate your assistance."

"No problem. Anytime you need someone to do a knock and talk on one of these, just give us a call."

"I will. And thanks again; have a great day, and you stay safe out there."

"Thanks, you do the same."

The two men shook hands and parted. Smith got into his vehicle and jotted down the time of departure from the suspect location.

"We are departing the area at approximately 1920 hours."

He then turned the ignition key, placed the car into drive, and gently pulled out of the parking space.

"Okay. Now I get to write another report."

Smith headed home. It was the end of his day. He would start the report writing in the morning.

CHAPTER TWO

More than Just Cable TV

Michael Smith was a long-term employee with Metro Cablevision. He started in the early 80's, working his way up from security guard to field service technician, to audit inspector, and eventually, field investigator. It was not much of a career path. In fact, the current job did not have any upward mobility at all. But he enjoyed what he did. At one time both he and his partner were police officers before joining the private sector. The thrill of being back on the *beat* was exhilarating

The cable business had changed over the years. Smith watched as new technology replaced the old. Ancient video sync suppression had been replaced with new digital video technology. Analog cable boxes were out, and new high-definition digital video recorders were in.

Smith had taken a few college courses

in computer networking to keep up with the changes in the business. With all the new products and services, like high-speed Internet and digital telephone, Smith knew that eventually he would become as obsolete as the analog descramblers that once were the terror of the cable TV industry. He had seen glorious days of high-profile sting operations, taking down large manufacturers of illegal cable decoders. But those days were long gone. Digital technology has taken care of that. Everything had now become *cyber*.

Smith glanced at his field investigation notes. His eyes scanned the computer monitor and set upon the tiny clock in the lower right-hand corner of the screen. It was 8:15 AM. Rolling the mouse, he moved the cursor across the screen and clicked on an icon to open his database. It was one of the few things that had survived the digital transition. Smith enjoyed tinkering with computer programs and had created a database (which he called *Cyber Cop*) in the mid-nineties. Several revisions had been made over the years, but the content always remained the same: bad guys stealing cable TV services. Now however, instead of illegal cable boxes, Smith and his partner were only investigating illegal cable hook-ups.

In a way it was easier to investigate illegal hook-ups because the connections were usually always outside with clear and open access. And the suspects were never paying subscribers. Investigating *black boxes* was a bit more complicated, because it required gaining access into the residence of a paying subscriber to verify that an illegal device was being used. That often posed a problem. But Smith and his partner had a rather good success rate, despite the complications that came with the investigation. It was always a challenge going to the door of a suspected illegal decoder user.

"The first fifteen seconds of the door contact will determine if you get it, or if they tell you to go pound sand."

Mark Stalwart was an ex-NYPD cop who moved to California in the late 70's. He had been hired by Metro Cablevision as a salesman but was quickly promoted to investigator when the company started up its cable TV theft of service program. Stalwart was eager to use his knowledge and skills as a police officer in the new position. The policies and procedures were cumbersome at first. But things somehow managed to get done. There were plenty of cases, but not very many arrests. Early on the company had taken the position that civil remedy was the best route to take against folks who stole cable TV services. Eventually, their position on the subject would change.

Smith transferred into the Network Security department as an auditor in the late 80's. Back then the department was known as *System Security*. Stalwart observed Smith closely and recognized he had an aptitude for investigations. He decided to take him along on a few door contacts to see if he really had what it took to be an investigator.

"Whatever you do," Stalwart had instructed, "do not let them know what you know, and especially don't let them know what you *don't* know. Just keep them guessing."

By the mid-nineties Smith was on the payroll as a full-time investigator. It was around that time that policies and procedures changed. Because of a snafu in one of their civil cases, Smith and Stalwart were told that cable thieves would have to be arrested and prosecuted criminally. That change presented certain logistical problems. For one, it required law enforcement officers to be on hand to affect arrests. That would mean contacting a dispatcher and requesting an officer, or a deputy to standby to preserve the peace. For most officers, this was a new experience. It took a lot of time educating the DA and various law enforcement agencies, but eventually, the process smoothed itself out.

Back in those days, Smith and Stalwart had a traveling "dog and pony" show. They would arrive early at police department briefings, armed with literature and hot-wired cable boxes for show-and-tell. Every police agency in the county was educated on the millions of dollars in lost franchise fees related to the multi-billion-dollar cable theft racket. Back then, raising the public's awareness of the economic impact was an integral component in the war on cable theft.

Smith was creative when it came to launching new concepts and thinking *outside the box*. He was innovative, always trying to stay on the cutting edge. He was one of the few cable investigators to first realize the power of the Internet as a potential tool for emerging cable pirates. The days of expensive magazine advertisement were rapidly fading. As the cheap construction of web sites and bulk email began to take hold, cable piracy became rampant. Realizing the need to counter their propaganda, Smith built an anti-piracy web site, which he called *UNCLENET*. He foresaw the need for the public and private sectors to communicate and share information, and so, he spent a great deal of time networking with law enforcement.

When Smith was not out chasing cable pirates or networking with federal agents, he was busy learning new computer programs that would help him improve the processes of his department. He had created *Cyber Cop* to keep track of the cases, making file updates and research relatively simple tasks. Every arrest was entered into the database. Reports were created for suspect profiles, case summaries, declarations, evidence chain of custody and restitution tracking. Smith had designed *Cyber Cop* specifically for his department's use, and it became a valuable tool.

He also designed many of the forms and documents, including the case narrative, which followed the regional law enforcement format. The case reports were packed with photographs, suspect statements, and minute details about the crime and the investigation. Deputy district attorneys had no problem prosecuting their *theft* cases.

Smith reviewed the notes in his field investigation report. He began to type the suspect's data into *Cyber Cop*.

"Seltzer, John David. Address, 5109 Via Torres, Oceanside 92057."

His thoughts were interrupted by the telephone ringing. He answered it.

"Metro Cablevision, Network Security, this is Michael Smith. How can I help you?"

"Mike, it's me, your buddy, Steve Gray over at the FBI."

"Steve, what's up?"

"You got a minute?"

"I sure do. How can I help you?"

"We have a situation, and we could really use your help."

"That's what I'm here for. Shoot."

"Right, well, I'm working on a case that involves one of your high-speed Internet subscribers."

"Oh boy, what the heck has happened now?"

"Well, as you know, I'm working with ICAC, the *Internet Crimes against Children* task force."

"I know."

"It seems that one or maybe more than one of your Internet customers have been accessing a European web site and downloading child pornography."

"I could have guessed."

"And, I have three IP addresses that come back to your company."

"Give them to me."

Special Agent Gray read the numbers as Smith jotted them down on a notepad with the words, "customer" "European web site" and "child pornography."

"Just give me a minute while I pull up the DHCP database," Smith said.

He pecked on the keyboard, inputting his username and password. The DHCP data was stored on servers at the corporate office, but

Smith had access to the information from his desktop. The program loaded, and he entered the first IP address.

"Okay. That IP address is not pulling up any information. The cable modem is either offline or the customer no longer has our service. Or there may be some other explanation."

"This information is kind of dated," Agent Gray explained. "We only recently got this case. It came through Interpol. They have been working on this for well over a year now. These IP addresses were recovered from access logs on the web server."

"I take it the web site is no longer up and running?"

"That is correct. It was shut down, and the computers were confiscated. Now we're following up on the end users who accessed the site and downloaded image files."

"I see. Steve, this may be a problem, but the DHCP database can only retrieve information as far back as six months. If those logs are any older than that, there is a strong possibility that the DHCP data will not point to the actual suspects."

"I understand. The logs show these particular IP addresses accessed the web site and downloaded JPEG images less than three weeks ago."

"Excellent. That makes me feel a whole heap more comfortable. I'd hate for you to go kicking in the front door of some poor unsuspecting, innocent person, and confiscating their hard drive; especially on information you get from me."

There was a restrained chuckle and then a long pause of silence, as Smith typed in the next IP address.

"Bingo! The second address is a hit. They are still current customers, and the DHCP data shows their IP has not changed in the last three months. They are good to go."

"Perfect."

"Hold on a minute, while I run the last number. Yes buddy, another positive, still using our service."

"Right on, this makes my job a whole lot easier."

"Okay bro', you already know the drill. I cannot release any subscriber information without a court order or subpoena. And of course, you'll need to fax it to our corporate legal department back in Atlanta."

"I'm on it, Mike. I will get an administrative subpoena signed and faxed off before lunch. Speaking of lunch, we need to get together. What does your schedule look like for next week?"

"I have a couple of meetings, but I might be able to squeeze in an hour or two for lunch. You are buying, right?"

"You bet."

"That's great. How does Thursday sound?"

"Thursday it is."

"Good, I'll see you then. By the way, include a comment on your fax cover page, and indicate that you and I have already spoken regarding this case. Let our paralegals know I have done the preliminary research on the IP addresses, and can package the information for you once they have received, reviewed, and approved the subpoena. That way we will expedite the info and get it to you more quickly. It makes sense to take the burden off our legal folks."

"You got it. See you next week."

Smith placed the receiver back onto the cradle, thinking about the cybercrime case his colleague was working on. In his mind's eye he visualized the images of innocent children, victimized over and over by pedophiles. He winced at the thought of young boys and girls missing from their homes, their families, and subjected to unspeakable torture. He felt compassion for those parents. How could they go on, knowing they may never see their child again?

He printed the DHCP data and customer information, secured the documents with a paper clip, and then set them on the stack of cases in his in-box. He sighed heavily and turned his attention back to *Cyber Cop*.

"One case at a time," he thought, "one case at a time."

He connected a USB cable from his digital camera to his PC and activated his image library program. He created a special folder to hold the case photos, and then uploaded the images to his computer.

He closed the image library window, and then carefully disconnected the camera and USB cable from his computer. He re-opened the window to *Cyber Cop* and imported the photo of Seltzer into the new data recorder. It took a few moments to for the database to link with the image library.

Smith completed inputting the suspect and arrest information into the database. He minimized the window, and then opened a new case narrative. Adding first the synopsis, then the origin of the investigation, he focused on the events that had transpired the day before. He began typing the narrative.

"On Tuesday, 18 October 2005, at approximately 1835 hours (6:35 PM) this investigator approached the above residence and attempted to make door contact. Prior to making contact I called the Oceanside Police Department and asked to have an officer standby and preserve the peace, while I conducted the investigation. The officer that responded was G. Barrymore, ID# 492. I briefed the officer on the case, the Penal Code section, and the procedures that I would follow.

"We approached the residence and made contact. A man, who later identified himself as John David Seltzer, answered the door. I asked him if he was the primary resident there, and he stated that he was. I identified myself as an investigator for Metro Cablevision and presented him with my photo identification. I explained the purpose of my visit and advised him that the officer was present as a precaution for my safety, and to preserve the peace. I asked for permission to enter, and permission was granted."

Smith paused for a moment, reflecting on some of the cases he and Stalwart had investigated together; in the days before the company adopted the policy of having law enforcement present to preserve the peace. He recalled one case where the suspect had threatened to shoot them at the door, and then released a pit bull on them. They had to run like hell to keep from being eaten. Another time, they entered a residence, only to observe loaded firearms and a huge Confederate flag hanging on the wall. They were both a bit uncomfortable during that interview, each for his own set of reasons.

Smith returned his attention to the case narrative and continued typing.

"We were escorted to the family room, where I observed a 32" Panasonic color television sitting inside an entertainment center. It appeared that the television was connected to Metro Cablevision cable services. It was on and tuned to Channel 53-Nickelodeon. I verified that the television was receiving all the cable channels by tuning to and viewing Channels 2 through 99.

"Seltzer stated that the cable service was working when they first moved in. I asked him how long he had resided there, and he stated, 'A little over a year.' Seltzer indicated they had moved into the residence in September of last year. I asked if there were other televisions in the house, and he stated, 'Yes.'

"We were escorted into the master bedroom, where I observed a 19" Sony color television mounted on the wall. The television was off. I asked for permission to turn it on and permission was granted. I observed that the TV was tuned to Channel 36-CNN. I verified that it was receiving all the cable channels by tuning to and viewing Channels 2 through 99.

"Seltzer led us to a small bedroom, which he indicated was the children's room. Upon entering I observed a 13" Sanyo color TV sitting on a chest of drawers. The television was on and was tuned to Channel 61-Cartoon Network. I verified that it was receiving all of the cable channels by tuning to and viewing Channels 2 through 99."

Smith clicked on the menu bar and inserted a data table into the document. He imported photographs of the televisions from his image library, which he had taken during the investigation. He added a caption beneath each photo, identifying the date it was taken, his name and ID number, and a brief description of what was depicted.

"I asked Seltzer if he knew how the cable had gotten reconnected. He stated that the cable had been working since they moved in. I asked him if he had ever noticed that the cable service went off, and he stated 'No.'

"I showed him photos that I had taken on 03 October 2005, which showed the illegal connection, and the way I left it after disconnecting the line. I asked him if he could explain how the cable got reconnected. He said that he could not explain it."

Smith inserted another table and imported photographs of the illegal connection outside in the cable pedestal. Again, he added captions, indicating the date, his name and ID, and a description of what was depicted.

"I asked him if he thought it was strange that he was receiving cable services without paying it. He said, 'Well, I guess so. I thought someone would eventually come out and disconnect it. I guess I really didn't think much about it.'

"I gave Seltzer a copy of California Penal Code 593d and read the section of the law that related to this case. I asked him if he agreed that intercepting cable services that he was not authorized to receive was a crime. He stated, 'Yes.'

"I placed Seltzer under citizen's arrest for violation of California Penal Code 593d. Officer Barrymore issued him a citation. He is scheduled to be arraigned in criminal court on 19 December 2005.

"We departed the area at approximately

1920 hours (7:20 PM)."

Smith added background information and the suspect statements to the document. He calculated the cost of the cable services had been received illegally and added the cost of the investigation. He completed a victim impact statement and included it with the case. He prepared duplicate copies; one set for his file and one set for the Oceanside Police Department. The officer would forward his crime case report to the DA along with Smith's narrative. That was the standard process.

Smith sat back in his chair and proofread the documents, looking for spelling and grammatical errors.

"Good case," he thought, as he printed two copies of the document.

He gathered the sheets together, took one set, and punched holes for a three-ring folder. He stapled the other set together and slipped it into a large white envelope. Later, he would deliver this copy to Officer Barrymore. He checked his email.

Smith clicked on the Microsoft Outlook icon on his desktop. The program opened displaying dozens of new messages in his inbox. Most of these were spam messages from unknown senders. The company's Information Technologies Department had installed spam filters on the network, but they did not help much. Junk email poured in daily from every corner of the globe with offers for male penis enhancements, low priced pharmaceuticals, and hot stock market tips.

Smith waded through the junk, highlighting clumps of messages, and deleting them.

"This is ridiculous," he thought, as he scrolled down the page.

There was an announcement from the Human Resources Department, reminding employees that it was time to complete their performance evaluations. Smith printed a copy of the message and placed it next to the keyboard. He continued scanning through the messages.

"Ah, here is something interesting, another theft report. Let us see what's happening here."

He opened the email message. It contained an attachment and a violation report. The message had come from the Customer Service Department. He read the contents. Someone had called in and reported a neighbor who was stealing cable TV service.

"'*Caller stated that the neighbor in Apt. E has spliced into the cable; wants to remain anonymous.*' They always want to remain anonymous. Friends and family cannot be trusted. If you ever decide to rob a bank, never tell friends or family."

In the sixteen years Smith had worked as an investigator for Metro Cablevision, he had seen reports from ex-husbands, ex-wives, ex-lovers, parents, children, friends, and neighbors, turning in the folks with whom they once had shared intimate relationships. Quarrels and breakups made them bitter and resentful, and even often got them involved as an *anonymous* call to the cable company. It never mattered if they had also enjoyed the free cable service for months or years. They just wanted revenge.

Smith added a case number to the report, and then printed a copy on his inkjet. He opened the customer database and input the account number listed on the violation report.

"So, we have a non-subscriber getting free

cable TV services. The last customer at this address was a Benjamin Cline. Service was disconnected in July of 2004. There have been no requests for service since that date."

Smith printed a copy of the customer data screen. He checked the house maintenance data for the map coordinates, and then he checked for any customer comments on the account. There were no outstanding bills, and the equipment had been returned. The account was clear of all bad debts. He closed the customer database.

He opened the Internet Explorer program and clicked on the fast link to Map Quest. He entered the address and waited for his map to load.

"Another one for Oceanside PD," he thought, as he printed a copy of the map.

Smith stacked the documents together, added a case cover sheet, and then paper clipped them together. He opened his binder and placed the new case inside. He then relaxed, sat back in his chair, folded his arms, and looked around the office. It was neat and clean. There were several award plaques from law enforcement organizations, including the FBI, mounted on the walls. Pictures of serene landscapes hung amongst the trophies. A smooth jazz melody played softly in the background, adding calm to the room, making anyone who entered feel right at home.

Smith reached across the desk and picked up the note from the Human Resources Department.

"Might was well get started on my evaluation."

He turned toward the computer and grabbed the mouse. He moved the cursor across the screen and clicked on a link to the Goals and Objectives web interface. He opened the program, clicked on the evaluation button, and reviewed his goals and objectives.

"This is going to be a half day project," he thought, pushing the mouse aside. "I'd better get my narrative over to OPD."

Smith stood up. He opened his notebook and placed the large white envelope inside next to the new theft case. He walked to the door and looked around, checking to be sure he was not forgetting something important. He switched off the light and closed the door behind him, locking it. The office and its contents were secured.

He walked down the corridor and out the front door. As he passed the security guard at the front desk, he nodded his head.

"I'll be out for a while, in case anyone is looking for me," he said.

"Okay. Have a good day."

"Thanks."

The morning air was exhilarating. Smith unlocked the Blazer and got inside. He placed the notebook on the passenger seat, adjusted his seat belt, and turned on the engine. He put a CD into the player and waited for the song to begin. He slowly backed the vehicle out of the parking space, shifted the car into drive, and headed toward the street. He made a right turn and proceeded toward the intersection.

The police station was only five miles from his office. Smith arrived there in less than fifteen minutes. He walked into the lobby and approached the front desk with the white envelope in hand.

"Can I help you?" asked the community

service officer.

"Yes. This narrative is for Officer Barrymore. Can you see that he gets it?"

"Sure, no problem, I'll put it in his inbox."

"Thank you."

Smith turned and walked out of the police station. He got back into his car and picked up the notebook. He opened it, took the new case out and looked it over.

"Okay, let's take a ride and see what we can find," he thought, while starting the engine.

Smith had no idea what to expect. He knew that every case was different; that some were complicated, while others were simple and straight-forward. He could never predict the outcome by just looking at the report. He would always drive by the address to get a visual of the residence, and possible locations where he could set up surveillance. The case might present a challenge, with the perpetrator living in an apartment building.

He pulled up to the address. The building was an old two-story structure with eight apartments. The wiring was external, making it vulnerable to pirating. Smith observed that the cable was lashed to the roof, bundled together, and fed down the wall into a locked box. There were several places where splicing could occur. He needed to get a closer look.

He parked the vehicle across from the apartment building. He put the digital camera into his pocket, removed his ID badge and got out of the car. It was almost noon. Most of the residents were out and about, either at work or out shopping. He entered the courtyard, quickly locating apartment E on the second level. His eyes followed the cable wires back to the locked box, but he could not find where the wires had been spliced. He approached the box, opened it with his security key and inspected the connections inside.

"Ah-h-h, there you are," he said, with a glimmer of satisfaction in his eyes.

It was a non-company splitter that connected the cable wires for apartments E and B to the direction tap. Smith knew the splitter was not authorized, and that unit E was receiving service illegally. But he did not know if unit B was an active customer, or just another cable thief. He called Field Service Dispatch.

"Communications Center, Dwayne speaking, how can I help you?"

"Hey Dwayne, this is Michael in Network Security."

"What can I do for you, Michael?"

"I'm out here at 4511 Delrina Drive in Oceanside. I have a theft of service case on unit E, and I need to know all the subscribers at this address. Can you tell me which units active and which ones are disconnected?"

"Sure, give me a minute to pull up the screen."

Smith looked at the cable wires inside the box, observing that unit E had an orange disconnect tag attached, marked with the date 7/11/04. He noted that the cable box had been locked with a special security key. Smith did not believe the resident had gained access to the cable box. Someone else had connected it for them, either a current employee or contractor, or someone who had been terminated. He looked at the two disconnected lines, units D and H. It appeared that the last recorded activity was the disconnection of unit H on 8/19/05.

The tech number indicated that a contractor had completed the job. Smith stored that date and tech number in his memory.

"Okay, here are the actives, units A, B, C, F and G. Units D, E and H are disconnected," reported the dispatcher.

"Thanks Gary. You've been a great help."

Smith put the cell phone away and turned his attention back to the cable wires inside the lock box. Units D and H were already disconnected. He took out his digital camera and photographed the unauthorized connection for apartment E. He placed the lid back onto the cable box and walked to his car. He opened the hatch, took out his tool belt and strapped it on. He walked back to the lock box, removed the lid, and proceeded to disconnect the cable line to apartment E. He placed two red audit tags on the line, upon which he marked his ID number and date of disconnection. He removed the illegal splitter and reattached unit B directly to the tap. He took photographs of the disconnected line, and then closed the lock box and secured it.

"Okay, my friend, I will come back and check on you in a few days."

Smith walked across the street, put the tools away and got back inside his vehicle. He pulled a new field investigation form from his notebook, filled in the address and case number, and wrote it into the log.

"Found drop active without billing, orange tag with illegal splitter; took photographs and disconnected line; attached red tags and secured lock box; recheck needed."

He started the engine, put the car into drive, and then gently pulled away.

"Now it's time to get something to eat."

Smith looked at the clock on the dashboard. It was 12:16 PM.

"Today is Wednesday; half-day for elementary school and Ruby won't be home. She'll be picking up Carolyn from school."

The drive home took all of ten minutes. He pulled into his driveway, leaving plenty of room for Ruby to pass with the family van and park inside the garage. They lived in a quiet gated community. The homes were less than four years old. Smith was fortunate to have bought the property when he did. Cost of housing had doubled since that time, and the value of his home was now well over seven hundred thousand. Smith looked around the cul-de-sac, admiring the landscape.

"Great neighborhood," he thought, turning to unlock his front door.

He entered, removed his shoes, and placed his keys on the bookcase near the entrance. He walked through the living room and into the kitchen.

"Hey little buddies," he said, approaching the fish tank and reaching for the tropical fish flakes. "I bet you're hungry, aren't you?"

Smith pinched off some flakes and scattered them across the water. A large goldfish swam to the top and quickly began to gobble the food. Several smaller fish picked off bits as they descended toward the bottom of the tank.

Smith walked into the laundry room and washed his hands. He returned to the kitchen and opened the refrigerator, took out a bag of salad, a package of roasted turkey breast slices and a small bottle of honey Dijon dressing. He removed a cutting board from the cabinet, placed it on the island, took a few turkey slices and cut them into thin strips. He poured out a generous portion of salad onto a plate, covered it with the turkey strips and added some honey Dijon dressing.

Smith sat down at the table to enjoy his meal. He heard the garage door open, and a few moments later, his six-year-old daughter bounded into the room.

"Hi Daddy, are you home for good, or do you have to go back to work?"

"Hey Pumpkin, no Daddy has to go back to work. Are you going to karate today?"

"I think so, if Mommy takes me."

At that moment Ruby walked through the door.

"Hi Michael, how is your day so far?"

"It's been pretty good, and what about yours?"

"Okay, I guess."

The couple had been together for almost twenty years. Their thirteen-year-old son, Michael Jr., was born the same year they were married.

"Did anything exciting happen at school today, Pumpkin?"

"Well, I got to move my frog all the way up to the top of the board."

"Your frog, you say? Wow that must have been really exciting."

"I was the only one who got to move my frog to the top of the board."

"And why was that?"

"It was because I knew the answer to the question about *atmosphere*."

"I'm very proud of you, Pumpkin."

Smith turned a puzzled look to his wife.

"She was listening to the teacher and paying attention," Ruby added, "and when he asked the question about atmosphere, Carolyn knew the answer. So, she got to move her frog to the top of the chart."

"Well, that's great," Smith said. "It's important to listen and pay attention when you're learning new things, Pumpkin."

"I know Daddy."

Smith smiled. It was hard for him to believe that his children were so grown up. Carolyn was already in first grade and Michael Jr. was in his last year of middle school.

"Time does fly, doesn't it?" he said, looking at Ruby.

"Yes, it does," she echoed.

Smith finished his lunch and pushed away from the table.

"I've got to go back to work," he said. "But some people are lucky. They get to stay at home."

Ruby grinned. She was a stay-at-home mom, having quit her job earlier in the year. Smith had been encouraging and convinced her to quit. He assured her that they could get by on his salary, and that the quality of life would improve for all of them, especially the children. Having her home in the mornings, preparing breakfast, and getting the kids off to school, and being there when they came home in the afternoon, was far more important than adding a few extra dollars to the savings account.

Ruby was at first reluctant to leave her employer with over fourteen years of service, but she trusted her husband's judgment. They made a lot of sacrifices, and somehow, they managed to get by.

"I'll see you guys later this evening," Smith said, giving his wife three quick kisses on the lips. "And you have a good time in karate class, Pumpkin. I love you."

He gave his daughter a big hug and kissed her on the forehead.

"See you later, Daddy."

Smith walked to the front door, picked up his keys and put on his shoes. Ruby and Carolyn followed him to the door. As he was leaving, he waved to them, and then he drove away.

CHAPTER THREE

What Gets Measured, Gets Done

"Goal number one, *'Provide support to local, state, and federal law enforcement agencies,'*" Smith muttered, looking over the goals and objectives of his evaluation.

He knew the self-evaluation was just a formality. In the final analysis, the security supervisor would determine if he had successfully met and exceeded the goals which had been established for him at the beginning of the year. *Proactive community relations* and *quality strategy* were key result areas that accounted for twenty-five per cent of his evaluation. He read the list of standards used to measure success for this goal.

'Assist leaders in law enforcement liaison; assist law enforcement agencies in crime investigations as needed and appropriate; assist task force effort in public awareness campaigns; continue to actively participate in law enforcement associations; provide updated training to local law enforcement.'

Smith spent a great deal of time interacting with law enforcement. As far as he was concerned it was one of the most important aspects of his job. Having the support and assistance of policemen, sheriff's deputies and federal agents was paramount to accomplishing all his goals and objectives. He knew that many other cable systems did not have the luxury of law enforcement support, because they had never taken the time to establish an interactive relationship. Smith began typing his self-evaluation.

'I am active in several law enforcement associations, including the HTCIA and the FBI InfraGard program. I frequently provide training to law enforcement agents who are new to cybercrime investigation, by bringing them up to speed on Company processes and procedures, and the fundamentals of computer networks.

'This overview is needed for the application of developing comprehensive and thorough search warrants when subscriber information is needed, as well as learning to effectively interact with the corporate legal department. Acting as liaison between the case agents and the legal department in Delaware, my close working relationship with law enforcement affords me the ability to expedite information in response to search warrants and subpoenas.

'I continue to serve as a steering committee member for the District Attorney's computer and technology crimes high-technology task force and have been tasked with the responsibility of developing a cyber security awareness program for small to medium size businesses in the area of Metro Cablevision's business services.'

Smith paused for a moment and reflected how he had been hoodwinked by the steering committee. At the last committee meeting a discussion had opened around cyber security issues, and the failure of small to medium-sized businesses

Devin Buchanan, the assistant US attorney had offered a suggestion to the committee that landed right in Smith's lap.

"Someone needs to accept the responsibility," Buchanan had stated, "and I think it is incumbent upon the ISPs that provide

Internet connectivity for small and medium-sized companies to get that message to those business owners. Cyber security is extremely important, and they have to take it more seriously."

Smith saw the ambush coming but was powerless to prevent it. Julia Hart, the committee chairperson, had quickly picked up on the direction Buchanan was headed, and turned her attention immediately to Smith.

"Well," she had stated in a rather cautious voice, "as you are the resident representative for ISPs on the board, could you look into that and report back to the committee?"

"Do I have a choice?" Smith had wanted to say, but instead he said, "Sure, no problem, I can handle that."

The project would become one of his goals for the upcoming year. It would require that he schmooze the right people within the company, but that did not matter. Smith had set his mind to accomplishing the task. He breathed a heavy sigh and returned his attention to the self-evaluation.

'I am also currently working with Dean

Vasquez in government relations to resolve key policy issues with Camp Pendleton base security, regarding business pass identification for Metro Cablevision field employees needing base access to conduct company business.'

"That should be enough," Smith said to himself. "I need a break."

He pushed himself away from the computer, stood up and stretched.

"I think I'll make myself a cup of tea."

Smith worked in a small office facility with slightly less than two hundred employees, eighty per cent of whom were field technicians. During most of the day only a handful of people populated the office. There was no cafeteria, only a small break room with free coffee and tea, and some vending machines. Smith got a Styrofoam cup from the cabinet and filled it with hot water. He dropped a tea bag inside and added three packets of sugar. He stirred the brew, and then took a sip.

"Excellent," he thought, as he made his way down the hall to his office. He sat down at his desk and placed the cup onto a coaster. The cherry wood furniture still looked new, even though it was several years old. Smith felt fortunate to have such a nice office.

"I can't complain too much," he said softly, "or they may decide to put me back into a cubicle."

It had taken the security department years to convince upper management that the investigators needed secure offices. The information in the cases they worked on was extremely confidential, and their case evidence needed to be locked away, secured from prying eyes. Evidence chain of custody was paramount, and Smith and Stalwart had plenty of cases pending criminal prosecution. Having secure offices made their job a whole lot easier.

"Goal number two, *'Resolve core video theft of service cases.'* Okay, another twenty-five per cent to cover *operational excellence* and *financial performance*."

Smith read the list of measurements.

'Investigate and/or resolve all theft of service cases in a timely fashion; close eighty per cent of new theft of service cases with twenty per cent continuing follow-up; assist corporate loss prevention effort in minimizing theft of service potential through proactive methods and procedures.'

Smith opened his database and printed a copy of all his resolved cases. He checked the case tracking program and highlighted all the cases that were assigned to him. He took a few moments to reflect the events of the past ten months, and then he began to type.

'Last year the number of service theft reports coming from field service dropped dramatically with the ramping up of the Techs Working from Home program. Early this year I decided to take a new approach, and, thinking outside the box, I implemented the Data Link Theft Report project. Together with the assistance of the information technologies department I developed a procedure by which field service techs could send email messages directly from their mobile data link terminals to my office desktop. The project has resulted in a dramatic increase in the number of service theft reports submitted by field service technicians. To date I have received seventy-five theft of core video service cases for the north county area. Of those cases, sixty-two have been closed and seven are pending court action (92%). The remaining six are active investigations with two being imminent door contacts.'

He read the section over, looking for grammatical errors. Achieving a case resolution of ninety-two per cent, well above the goal, could potentially score Smith an 'exceeds' in that category. Luckily, he was never evaluated on the number of arrests or criminal prosecutions. Stalwart was always the highest achiever in that category. Smith continued typing.

'In keeping with the will and direction of corporate security, my leaders requested in April of this year that I learn and evaluate the new corporate security database for possible implementation in our local risk management program.'

He paused for a moment, thinking back to the conversation he had with the security supervisor and the manager of risk management.

"If you want me to look at the program," Smith had stated during their meeting, "I'd be glad to evaluate it and give you my feedback."

"All the systems are being asked to use this new security database," David Newell, the manager of risk management, had added, "and I just want to be ahead of the game."

"I just have some concerns about the type of information we will be adding to this database," Smith confessed. "We don't know who will have access to it. Right now, we are using Cyber Cop to house all our criminal case records. It is local, and it's secure. No one has access to it except us. I don't know that the same can be said for a database that's being shared by other cable systems."

"I don't think we should stop using Cyber Cop," interjected Simon Butcher, the security supervisor. "We just need to add basic information to the corporate database."

"That may also require duplication of effort," Smith noted, "depending upon how much data we will be inputting."

"We don't want to duplicate our efforts," Newell stated. "We'd be spending all our time inputting data and wouldn't be getting much production done."

"I'll look at it," Smith asserted, "and give you my feedback."

The corporate security database was exceedingly complex and covered a wide variety of incident and case types; unlike *Cyber Cop* which had been created for a specific type of case. For all it was designed to do it was not capable of producing aggregate data reports, which was exactly what risk management needed. Smith continued typing.

'I corresponded with corporate security and learned the nuts and bolts of the database program. Upon completion of the evaluation, I presented an overview of the database and its functional components to my leaders. I assisted the corporate security staff in scheduling classroom instruction on the database program for the entire risk management team. The corporate security database has been implemented locally in our system.'

He sat back and reviewed the self-evaluation.

"I wonder how this will fly," he said to himself, "now that both the security supervisor *and* the manager of risk management are unhappy with the corporate security database and all of its shortcomings."

It was true. Since the very beginning there were problems with the database. It was offline most of the time with server problems, which made critical case data inaccessible to the local systems. And besides corrupting records occasionally, there was also the problem with the inadequate reports it produced.

Smith realized this drawback might hurt his chances of getting an "exceeds" in this category, even though it wasn't his fault that the database didn't perform the way the local system wanted it to. He had done exactly what his leaders requested of him, to learn and evaluate the program.

"No matter," he said, "it was an important project, despite the problems."

Smith looked at the next goal.

"'Provide effective communication with all Metro Cablevision employees regarding reporting theft of service cases, etc.' Another twenty-five per cent goes to quality strategy and customer relationship."

Setting goals and objectives was an important part of the business. It allowed the senior management team to observe the metrics of each department and evaluate the effectiveness of its leadership. Not everything that was *done* got measured, but everyone made sure that everything that was *measured* got done.

'Continuous feedback to employees on resolved theft of service cases; update customer service representatives on procedures for network security and theft of service reporting; provide training and policy updates to field service technicians and customer service representatives on network and information security; generate recognition for employees' theft of service support.'

Smith and Stalwart were diligent about providing feedback to employees. Everyone was curious to find out what had happened with the report they submitted. In years past the investigators had often written 'sanitized' versions of their case narratives for the company newsletter. But neither Stalwart nor Smith had submitted anything for publication in a long time.

'I have attended and presented important information and updates to field service technicians during team training, including Reporting Violations on Camp Pendleton and the Data Link Theft Report project. I also have taken the opportunity to use various department meetings to recognize employees for their contribution and support of the theft of service program. The Security Recognition Award has been a huge success and has made a tremendous difference this year in the quantity and quality of the theft of service reports received from field technicians. Employees from field service and network operations have been recognized for helping our department achieve its goals. By continuously providing feedback to employees and/or their supervisors on resolved theft of service cases, we have developed a great rapport with the departments responsible for generating most of our cases. To improve the quality of information recorded in theft of service reports, I submitted an updated version of the Violation Report to the customer service department earlier this year to be posted on their electronic bulletin board. I have seen evidence that customer service representatives are using the new form in several reports I have received from the customer service department.'

Smith sat back and rubbed his eyes. He looked at the clock on the computer. It was 3:05 PM.

"One more," he said, moving closer to the keyboard. "Goal number four, *'Resolve high technology crime cases.'*"

This final category accounted for the remaining twenty-five per cent of Smith's evaluation and covered *'quality strategy'* and *'financial performance.'* He read the list of measurements.

'Investigate and/or resolve all Internet and computer-related crime cases in a timely fashion; close eighty per cent of new cybercrime cases with twenty per cent continuing follow-up; assist law enforcement investigations through data research and report generation in compliance with search warrants, court orders and subpoenas.'

Smith looked at the documents he had printed out earlier in the day during his phone conversation with Special Agent Gray. He started typing.

'I am currently working with investigators

from the District Attorney's computer and technology crimes high-tech task force, the FBI and other law enforcement agencies across the country, assisting in investigations of Internet-related crime, including credit card fraud, identity theft, auction fraud and various other cybercrimes. I contribute to these investigations by conducting preliminary DHCP database research and acting as liaison between the case agents and the Metro Cablevision legal department in Delaware. My close working relationship with law enforcement affords me the ability to expedite information in response to search warrants and subpoenas. To date a total of twenty-one cybercrime cases originating from law enforcement agencies have been logged into our case tracking system. All cases have been closed with one hundred per cent successful resolution.'

He read over the self-evaluation and corrected a few grammatical and typographical errors. He saved the file and printed a copy for his records.

"Now I'll send the boss an email message and let him know that I've completed my evaluation."

Smith drafted the email, sent it to the security supervisor, and forwarded a blind carbon copy to his own email address for archiving. He opened the desk drawer, shuffled through the green hanging folders until he found the file he was looking for, *Evaluations and Personal Data.*

Smith opened the file folder and pushed the papers back.

"What's this?" he asked himself, retrieving a roughly typed document. It appeared that he had written it on *February 20, 1992.* "I vaguely remember writing this," he said, as he started to read.

'I begin this formal documentation today. There are several reasons for this. During my explanation, I will attempt to place events and dates in order, so that the pattern of discrimination can be better understood.'

Smith paused. The document was almost fourteen years old. It was entitled 'Discrimination Documentation.' He continued reading.

'I have worked for Metro Cablevision for

over seven years. During my employment, I have worked in the capacity of security officer, field service technician, auditor, investigator, and most recently, as audit inspector.

'My present supervisor, Simon Butcher, has made me realize just how fragile my employment with Metro Cablevision really is. During a recent interaction, a private meeting on January 31, 1992, Butcher informed me that even though the job classification for my position of auditor was being upgraded from a level six to a level seven, and reclassified as an audit inspector, I would not receive a pay increase. The rest of the field personnel in my department, however, did receive a five per cent pay increase.

'Butcher, acting on behalf of manager William Drake, defended his position by asserting that both he and Drake had discussed my particular situation, and had determined that I should not be increased in salary for the following reasons:

'Early in 1990, around the middle of February, I received a promotion to investigator, which was a salaried position at pay level eight. During the initial training period, which lasted more than six months, I was asked to perform additional duties, beyond the actual job description of investigator, i.e., assisting the field service department with disconnections and installations of cable service. This I did.

'My work, however, as a field investigator was no less than exceptional. I assisted in door contacts and performed all the required responsibilities of a field investigator. Moreover, I exceeded in the production required in my job evaluation.'

Smith looked around his office, and sighed heavily, remembering the early days when nothing was certain, and no one could be trusted.

'The promotion to field investigator came at a time when the audit department was in a precarious situation. The department had been targeted by upper management to be eradicated. Slowly, the audit crew was placed into other positions in the company, until there remained only one auditor, Christopher Long.'

Chris Long had been one of the hardest working auditors in the crew. He got along well with most people, but occasionally got under some folks' skin. Long, who was just two years younger than Smith, had died of cancer in February of 2004. Smith kept a copy of the memorial edition of the company newsletter in his office; to remember him, his smile, and his happy, infectious spirit. A lot of words could be used to describe him. Smith brushed a tear from his eye, as the word *friend* came to mind. He cleared his throat and started reading again.

'Butcher and Drake pursued management to review the statistics relative to cable piracy and the overall penetration of our service area. They pointed out the fact that the audit department was responsible for locating unauthorized active cable lines, terminating the service, and subsequently generating incremental sales and new cable customers.

'In mid-September 1990, I was called into Drake's office, accompanied by my supervisor, Butcher. In this private session I was informed in a very impersonal and blatant manner that my position as field investigator was being dissolved, and effectively immediately, I would resume my job duties as an auditor.

'Drake, in an almost defiant tone, announced that I would retain the title of investigator and remain a salaried employee until the first of the year 1991. He further indicated that, under normal circumstances, I would be decreased in salary by five per cent, because of the job change to a lower position.

'I must interject at this point with an especially important note:

'I was given the position of field investigator when the post was vacated by Stewart Valentine. I was told at that time that I was the most qualified candidate for the job, given my extensive background in security and law enforcement. Drake and Butcher were anxious for me to get started in my new position as investigator and rushed the paperwork through the channels. Everyone agreed with my selection to the position, from my supervisor right up to the vice president of community relations. Without a doubt everyone agreed that I was the most qualified candidate for the position.'

Smith rubbed his chin, thinking back on how quickly those same people had turned against him, even his partner, Mark Stalwart. Something had happened that caused them to change, but he could not remember what it was.

'When the promotion documents reached

the desk of Roger McDougal, Metro Cablevision's general manger, however, there suddenly developed a profoundly serious dilemma. McDougal was not satisfied with my selection to the position. He asked Drake and Butcher if they were sure they wanted to go through with the promotion. Apparently, the alternative he gave them was to get by with one investigator; something that had never been done for certain obvious reasons. All contacts with individuals committing cable theft must be witnessed by at least two Metro Cablevision employees for legitimacy; and so that the information in the narrative report is accurate to the letter with the events that transpired during the investigation and interview with the suspects.

'Consequently, I was called into Drake's office after the fact. Drake said in a most embarrassing manner, that he had both good news and bad news with relation to my job promotion. The good news was that after tedious communication with McDougal, the promotion papers were finally signed. However, the bad news was that the promotion would not go into effect until about the first week of March.

'At this point I felt both relief and outrage. I did not speak with anger, even though my heart was stricken. I could see the embarrassment in both Drake's and Butcher's eyes. Both avoided direct eye contact with me. I knew at this point that I must prove beyond any shadow of a doubt that I was worthy of the promotion.

'Little could have prepared me for the meeting in Drake's office some six months later, when I would be told that my position as a field investigator was to be dissolved.

'Despite my job performance (and in fact I was commended on the great job that I had done), I was being reduced to the position of auditor. Drake was articulate and precise in his presentation, as he attempted to make me feel that he and Butcher were doing me a great service by not penalizing me with a five per cent reduction in pay.

'He further emphasized that my skill as an auditor was more valuable and important at this time than my job as an investigator. For a while, Butcher assisted Mark Stalwart, the remaining investigator, with door contacts. I therefore resumed my duties as an auditor.

'In this September 1990 meeting, Butcher and Drake asserted that they had finally succeeded in convincing upper management that the audit department was an asset for the company. They had been given a green light to begin rebuilding the audit crew.'

Smith recalled those events clearly. The senior team had chosen to increase the field service department at the expense of the audit team. They rationalized that the field service technicians could install service and audit the system at the same time. They had been wrong. When the net gain statistics came in for the months of July and August, the unprecedented drop was more than alarming. The senior team racked their brains trying to figure out what had happened. When Butcher and Drake explained it to them for the umpteenth time, they finally got it. Net gain was directly affected by systematic, street-by-street, tap-by-tap audit of the cable system. Management had made an unbelievably bad business decision when they dismantled the audit crew. He continued reading the document.

'Meanwhile, Chris Long and I would carry the burden of proof that audit was solely responsible for a fair share of the company's incremental sales.

'As I attempted to pull my life back into

focus, I was haunted by the memory of my first meeting with Drake and Butcher, when I was told that McDougal almost did not approve my promotion. For me this was simply the day after. Being stripped of my post was an indisputable embarrassment to me.

'I reflected how, during my training period, Butcher constantly avoided answering my questions whenever I inquired about the length of my training. His response was always the same, "I'll let you know." At those times he avoided eye contact and appeared irritated and distracted. I would not press him for a definite date or time when I would be considered a full-fledged investigator.

'Instead, when the period was over, so was my job as an investigator. I realized that my career in the audit department was at a dead end, and I began to watch the job board for a position that I would qualify for. Miraculously, two positions opened at the same time.

'One job, editor of the company newsletter, was filled by a white female from outside the company. I had been told by Butcher, prior to the selection for the position, that the vice president of community relations was looking for a woman to fill that job. Apparently, Butcher knew much more about company politics than he was willing to admit.

'The other position, field services trainer, was filled by a white male. This was most disturbing in the fact, that the personnel department had decided to lower the minimum qualifications, thereby indicating that the position was intended for someone specific.'

Smith chuckled, remembering the two people who were selected for those positions. Both had been horrible in those jobs, and both quit without notice. After twenty years, he was still a faithful employee.

"Another case of management making bad business decisions," he smirked, turning the page of the document, and continuing.

'Being discouraged at the obvious process that was taking place, I decided to bide my time and concentrate my energy on maintaining my present employment.

'I was further hindered by the fact that I failed my pole climbing certification test, even though my climb was the best I had ever done. I watched as others climbed, breaking established rules of pole climbing, and were given passing marks, because the committee decided to change the established rules in certain situations. (Chris Long, for example, never locked his knees while climbing. But I failed because the committee said I looked shaky.)

'By this time, I realized that I was purposely being singled out. Why? Only Butcher and Drake know the answer to that. How far up the ladder did it go? I cannot possibly know. Yet, from the series of events that had transpired, I knew that more than just a few individuals were bearing ill-will toward me.

'Regardless, I continued to perform my job duties. The audit department head count was being increased, and I tried to put the negative events behind me. But there were numerous disappointments and reminders.

'Early in 1990, I had created a video for the personnel department to be used as an overview in the initial employment screening of field service technicians. Expecting compensation, I asked the personnel department to evaluate the tape, which they eagerly used, duplicated, and distributed. I was informed later, however, that the committee could not set a monetary value on the videotape, and therefore could not award me anything in return. I was presented with a certificate of appreciation on May 7, 1990.

'Knowing employees who had presented simple ideas and suggestions and received thousands of dollars in compensation, I was crushed when all I got was a piece of paper that basically said thanks.'

Smith had written this document during a period when he was under fire from management and feared that he would be wrongfully terminated. He reflected over his years of service with the company. He had been subjected to a great deal of abuse from his leaders *and* co-workers.

"I just couldn't let them beat me," he muttered, clinching the paper. "I had to prove that I was stronger, mentally and emotionally."

He read on.

'By the time my position as investigator had become a memory, Butcher approached me with a request; a request that reopened the wounds and poured salt into them.

'He had grown weary of assisting Stalwart with door contacts and had discussed with Drake the feasibility of having me take on the responsibility. There would be no change of job status, no pay increase and I would be required to work nights one day out of the week. This I would do in addition to my job duties as an auditor. Numbed by the previous circumstances, I inquired about the night differential, which normally applies to such split shift schedules. Butcher flatly stated there would be no shift differential because Drake could not see paying me an additional seventy cents an hour, simply to work one night a week. Besides, they had arranged for me to work from 11:30 AM to 8:00 PM, which would cancel any shift differential that I would normally be entitled to.

'I became annoyed at this and told Butcher that it was outrageously unfair and possibly illegal. Apparently, it was unjust, because he later informed me that Drake had changed his mind about the shift differential. Butcher blamed himself for probably not explaining it correctly to Drake the first time.

'Despite the newly imposed responsibilities

and demands placed upon me as a part-time auditor / part-time investigation assistant, I was required to participate in installation and disconnect campaigns for the field services department.

'During one such blitz I was given a packet of discrepancy disconnects to complete. *Butcher* told me that some people in the field services department had concerns about me. They felt that I was not capable of performing the job and did not want me to participate in the program. He said they told him I was not worth the effort. Butcher said he assured them that I could do the work.

'Having worked in field service I am aware of how packets of disconnects are put together and routed. Discrepancy disconnects are jobs that have been kicked back by other technicians because they were too difficult to complete. Every job I had was located at the top of a gaff pole. Not being gaff certified I had to use my twenty-eight-foot ladder to reach the cable equipment. By noon I was nauseous, suffering from heat exhaustion. About an hour and a half later I became dizzy and started to pass out. The combination of heat exhaustion and physical stress had placed me into a precarious situation. I had completed eleven disconnects in the packet. I left the field and returned to the shop. I told Butcher that I was ill and did not feel safe continuing to carry and climb the twenty-eight-foot ladder. He was not sympathetic but did allow me to go home early.

'The next morning Butcher handed me another packet of disconnects. He told me that I had embarrassed him and the entire audit department and ordered me to complete the new packet of disconnects. There was no recourse. I was told that I would complete the packet of disconnects, or else. There was no consideration. He was totally disrespectful. I completed the packet of disconnects.

'Two days ago, Butcher told me that Jake Allen, another auditor, had completed fourteen jobs during one of the blitz days. Butcher said that was acceptable because Allen had been given a packet of discrepancy disconnects that no one else wanted to do. I did not say anything.

'Despite any appearance of fairness, I knew that Butcher was deceitful, dishonest, and biased. During a private conversation on January 31, 1992, Butcher informed me that I would not be receiving the five per cent pay increase with the rest of the department. He had stated the reason was because I did not get a pay reduction when I was demoted from the position of investigator back to auditor. I told Butcher this was just another item in a long list of embarrassments that I have had to endure.

'He responded, "How is this an embarrassment? No one will ever find out about it unless you tell them."

'I said that I knew somehow the information would leak out, and I would again face humiliation and embarrassment. He was adamant, stating, "Regardless, no one will find out unless you tell them."

'On February 14, 1992, I was married. I took a four-day weekend and returned to work on February 18. I got a copy of the company newsletter and discovered that the information concerning the pay increase had been made public. I saw that all the auditors had been promoted, except me. I was named as a transfer. It was clear from the context that I had not been promoted. Later, I overheard one of my co-workers make the comment, "Michael didn't get a raise."

'When I brought this to Butcher's attention,

he simply shrugged his shoulders and said in a detached voice, "I am sorry that it happened. Somebody messed up. I'll go and have a talk with personnel."

'Later that morning, Lisa Schwartz, a representative from personnel, spoke to me and said that if I wanted to vent, she would listen to what I had to say. Not trusting her or anyone else in the company, I avoided the subject. She pursued it saying, "I am an employee advocate." It was clear that more was going on than what appeared on the surface.

'She continued, saying, "I have been there since the beginning of all this." She was referring to my demotion from investigator to auditor. "When I read the newsletter," she said, "I was upset. I asked myself, how would I feel if I were Michael?"

'I did not reveal my feelings to her, but instead, smiled and said that this was just another event that would pass with time. I would not confide in her or anyone else in the company, because I knew they could not be trusted. So, I resigned myself to calm silence, and began this journal.

'I feel that the people I work for have

violated my right of privacy. They have violated my human and civil rights. I will continue to maintain this journal in case it becomes necessary for a future discrimination lawsuit.'

Smith sat back in his chair.

"Damn," he said aloud. "What the hell was going on back then?"

A sense-memory came to him. And, for a few moments he was back in 1992, feeling all the emotional stress brought on by the uncertainty of his employment situation. He had learned not to trust anyone, and he felt detached and alone. Looking at the clock on the computer, he saw that it was 3:23 PM.

CHAPTER FOUR

Okay, So Now You Need Me

"Is everything okay?" asked Joe Blackwell, poking his head into Smith's office.

"Yeah, everything's fine. How did you do in the field today? Did you find a lot of U.A. connections?"

Blackwell was an audit inspector and spent his days checking non-subscriber addresses for unauthorized cable connections. He occasionally worked with Smith on service theft investigations.

"I did pretty well," said Blackwell as he sat down in the chair nearest the door. "I found eleven unauthorized active drops and three missing traps."

"That's good. Is there anything I can go out on right away? Someone I can arrest for cable theft?"

"No, there's nothing you can go on right away. But I have a couple of situations that is promising. I will just have to check them out again in a few days to see if they have decided to hook themselves back up. What are you working on?"

"I just finished my job evaluation. This morning I completed my narrative report for the arrest I made yesterday and then dropped it off at OPD. I went out on a new theft of service case, found the line active without billing, took photographs and disconnected it. Funny thing is though; the illegal splitter was connected inside the locked box. I'm guessing that a contractor was out making himself some extra cash on the side."

"Do you have any suspects?"

"Not exactly; but the last person that was inside the box before today was a contractor. He disconnected one of the other units and may have illegally hooked up the suspect while he was there. I have his tech number and the date he was there. It was written on the orange disconnect tag."

"That sounds interesting. It would be nice

to lock up a scumbag contractor. You could make an example of him, so other contractors won't go out and do the same thing."

"Well, it's not that simple. There is no way to tell at this point if the contractor did it, or if someone else made the illegal connection. I have to gather more information before I make assumptions about who did what."

"Yeah, yeah, I know. But you and I both know that all contractors are crooked scumbags."

"Sorry, but I can't agree with that. For me to conduct an effective investigation I have to keep an open mind and stay objective."

"Sure, you do. You're just trying to stay politically correct."

"That too, but honestly, I can't make any judgments about guilt or innocence until I have enough evidence to prove one way or the other."

Blackwell smirked, shrugged his shoulders, and slumped further down in the chair. He was about half Smith's age. Working on a bachelor's degree in business management, Blackwell was planning to move up the company ladder and into a management position.

"Well, I have to finish my paperwork and clock out," he said, rising slowly from his chair. "They don't want us to get any more overtime this year, and it's just about 3:30."

Smith glanced at the tiny clock on the computer screen for a moment, and then turned his gaze back onto Blackwell. "You're right Joe," he said, "I don't want you getting into trouble with your supervisor. See you tomorrow."

Blackwell walked out of the office and down the hall. Smith sat back in his chair and looked up at the bulletin board mounted on the wall above his desk. It was divided into two sections. The erasable white board had the names of defendants and dates of pending and closed court cases written neatly on it.

"My next court date is December 19th," he said quietly to himself; "case number 05-04-104N, Department 14. He'll probably plead not guilty and ask for a court appointed attorney."

Smith was used to dealing with defense attorneys and was no stranger to the criminal justice system. He had been called to witness in numerous thefts of service cases, and always presented a professional demeanor while under oath. Many of the public defenders in North County knew him and his reputation for writing thorough reports. One attorney even commented, "Your reports are more detailed than a lot of the murder cases that come through here. And they're better written than most of the police reports I've seen." Smith took it as a compliment.

Two newspaper articles were posted on the push-pin section of the bulletin board next to the list of pending court cases. Smith had placed them there as a reminder that he really was making an impact in the cable industry through his efforts to deter signal theft. He believed that more publicity was needed to raise community awareness and had suggested that the company air public service announcements regarding the effects and consequences of cable theft. The suggestion simply withered on the vine. It seemed that even though management was highly motivated to increase subscriptions and subsequent net gain, no one seemed willing to publicly raise the issue of cable theft.

Smith read the headline on the first article.

"Cable Theft Suspects Arrested."

He continued.

"Metro Cablevision agents arrested 13 people Sunday morning on suspicion of stealing television cable service at a Vista apartment complex, authorities said.

"Five altered cable boxes were seized out of 16 units checked in a Sumac Road complex formerly known as the Margarita Apartments, said sheriff's Cpl. Stan Mason.

"Cablevision representatives made citizen's arrests on suspicion of misdemeanor theft of cable services, and then released the 13 suspects. The maximum penalty is six months in jail and a $1000 fine.

"'We were just there to preserve the peace,' Mason said.

"One person was cited for suspected possession of a small amount of marijuana and released.

"Cable theft drives up the cost for all customers, said Michael Smith, a Cablevision investigator. The National

Cable Telecommunications Association in Washington, D.C. estimates cable theft nationally at $6.5 billion a year.

"In addition to stealing basic cable service, Smith said, some suspects allegedly altered it to include additional services, such as premium movie channels."

The news story was over two years old. The next article was more recent but did not deal with cable theft at all. The headline read, "Woman Arrested in Identity Theft."

Smith continued.

"A 29-year-old woman was arrested yesterday on suspicion of identification theft and credit card fraud for placing fraudulent orders over the Internet.

"Grace Wheeler, a former temporary employee of a telecommunications company, was booked into Las Colinas Women's Detention Facility with a bail set at $175,000, investigators of the District Attorney's Office said yesterday.

"Wheeler was arrested after investigators from the DA's Computer and Technology Crime High Tech Response Team and Identity Theft

Suppression Task Force searched her apartment, District Attorney Brenda Dunn said in a news release.

"Investigators said they seized documents indicating that Wheeler had been placing fraudulent orders over the Internet for more than 18 months. The investigation began when Metro Cablevision workers reported to the district attorney that Wheeler attempted to pay her cable television bill with stolen credit card information. Wheeler is scheduled to be arraigned in San Diego Superior Court Monday."

Smith had gone out on the early morning raid with Task Force investigators. He recalled the expression on Wheeler's face, as she sat handcuffed on her sofa. Even as the investigators uncovered piece after piece of criminal evidence, she denied doing anything wrong. Had she not attempted to pay her cable bill with stolen credit card information, she may have gone undetected forever. Smith chuckled.

"This is one to remember," he mused.

A message icon popped up on his computer monitor. He checked the inbox and saw that the email was from Simon Butcher, the security supervisor. He opened the message and read the contents. It was a security alert dealing with vehicle break-ins. Several laptop computers had been stolen from field service units, and the Security department was given the priority to take steps to prevent more thefts.

Butcher advised all Metro Cablevision employees to remove the laptops from their vehicles and secure them in their homes, while off-duty. The message went on to instruct employees to write down and secure the serial and model numbers of the devices in the event they were lost or stolen.

"Same stuff as before," Smith mused as he recalled events fourteen years prior.

Shortly after his demotion back to field auditor, Smith was asked to assist Stalwart on his theft of service cases. Butcher did not like being involved directly in field investigations and convinced the Risk manager to pass the task on to Smith. There was a great deal of conflict within the department back then. Smith's duties were split between audit and investigations, two distinctly different types of jobs, and his work suffered as a result.

His audit routine was constantly being interrupted by field investigations. But then, something very unusual happened in the spring of 1994. A series of vehicle break-ins occurred, and dozens of analog cable boxes were stolen. The Security department was given the task of tracking down the perpetrators, or at the very least, find a way to stop the thefts.

Smith was pulled from his audit duties and assigned to help with the investigation. After a few weeks, the company decided to reactivate him as a full-time investigator.

Smith remembered thinking at that moment, "*Oh, so now you need me.*"

It was not the ideal circumstances under which Smith wanted the job back, but at least, he was reinstated. The email message reminded him how nonchalant management had been when he suggested installing tracking software on all company laptop computers in the event they were lost or stolen.

Two years prior when the company announced that all field service units would be equipped with state-of-the-art mobile computer systems, the project coordinator sent an email to the Security department requesting input on processes and procedures. Smith received the notice second hand from his manager and responded promptly. He carefully reviewed the original email message that was sent to his manager.

It read,

"We have already deployed 26 Panasonic laptops in the North Network Operations trucks and will be placing them in 40 South Network Operations vehicles. Going forward, we will be placing 100 more of these computers in field service trucks before the end of the year and more over the next few years. The price of each machine is about $3200. These computers are full laptops as opposed to the 'tablet' computers we are currently using. This makes them more useful and a more enticing target for theft. The computers are in lockable docks in the truck with each dock individually keyed. Master keys are available which are currently used by those of us who service the computers and radio equipment. I am requesting some guidance from the Security Department on issues you may see with expensive equipment with a consumer value in the trucks. Some of the items we are concerned about are:

- Recognizing that managing individual keys is a challenge, we are considering giving each technician a master key.
- The keys have a proprietary blank available

only from Panasonic.
- The current tablet computer docks are master-keyed and no problems with theft have been encountered.
- Since this key would open the Panasonic docks in all Metro Cablevision trucks (as well as docks in all local telephone company vehicles) is this a good plan?
- If we do provide this key, how do we assure it is returned at the end of employment? What if it is not returned?
- Techs Working from Home, Network Operations on-call, North County field service vehicle take-home program; places these computers at the technicians' home overnight. How can we mitigate that exposure?
- The wording of the document signed by the technician when the equipment is issued. Sample attached which has been signed by the North Network Operations technicians.
- Thank you for your consideration of this situation."

The note was signed by the project coordinator. Smith's manager, David Newell, had forwarded the email message to Butcher and him with a short note, *"Michael, Simon...I would like your input here."*

Smith understood more about computers and computer crimes than anyone in his department, and at that time, probably the company. He never considered himself a "guru" or "computer geek," but he kept abreast of crimes involving computers and computer networks. He had established himself within the cybercrime law enforcement community and was active in several high technology crime associations.

He had responded to the email request with a detailed recommendation that began,

"I suggest that in addition to the accountability and policy solutions that you look into software solutions as well. Please look at the info below and the attached URL."

His message described in simple terms how computer systems attach to the Internet with a unique identifier called an IP address. He went on to explain how the tracking software worked.

The project coordinator responded back,

"Michael, I appreciate your input on this. However, the radio network we utilize does not allow this type of tracking. The computers do not have IP addresses. We have documented the serial number of the computers and could include the MAC address of the NIC. I am looking to the Security Department to consider physical security of the computers in the vehicles such as locking procedures, solid, enforceable documentation signed by the employee, and confirmation that existing company policies are adhered to by the employees when the vehicle is at the employee's home overnight."

Smith chuckled.

"Of course, the radio network doesn't allow Internet access," he mused. "The software would only be necessary if the computer has been stolen. Anyone who has a free laptop will eventually use it to connect to the Internet. That's when the software will be useful… helping us to track it down and get it back."

But the software was never installed, and the suggestion faded into the backdrop, as did most of the ideas that were presented by front-line employees like Smith. The problem (obvious to some but not to most) was that the suggestions came from people who were far more knowledgeable than those making the decisions. And during the two years that followed over two dozen laptop computers were stolen from the company; half of those were taken right out of the warehouse. No one seemed to understand why Smith had suggested installing the tracking software. He shook his head and sighed.

"Here we go again," he said, as he opened the desk drawer and pulled out a colleague's business card.

"Time to give Jack a call," he thought.

Jack Stuart was the Director of Investigations and Recovery for Cyber-Trace, a Canadian company that specialized in computer tracking software. Smith had worked with Stuart in the past on several investigations involving stolen computers. The tracking software that had been installed on the machines allowed Cyber-Trace to remotely locate the devices when they connected to the Internet. The computers, in a sense, "phoned home" to Cyber-Trace broadcasting their serial numbers, MAC addresses, host names and IP addresses. Security personnel collected the data, contacted the Internet service providers where the "call" originated, and notified the local law enforcement agency. Once the ISPs identified the subscribers associated with the IP addresses, local police armed themselves with search warrants, and moved on the suspect locations.

Often, the individuals on the receiving end were totally unaware that the laptop they had in their possession had been stolen. It was common for Internet users to purchase computers through online auctions, like eBay. And it was just a matter of time before they were connected to the Internet. Fortunately for the end-users, the devices were simply confiscated and returned to the proper owners. They lost the money they had spent to purchase the equipment; but for law enforcement, it was just another step in the investigation. More documents would be uncovered, new usernames, Internet accounts and IP addresses would have to be researched; and more search warrants would be written, issued, and executed. It was a long process, but eventually, the perpetrators would be caught.

Smith understood the process and had advised management that it would be prudent to equip every company laptop with tracking software. But in the usual fashion, they dismissed his suggestion as being *"not relevant to business needs."* He shook his head and sighed.

"I'll give Jack a call and see if we can't help to mitigate some the damage," he said to himself, picking up the phone and dialing the number on the business card. The phone rang on the other end, and someone picked it up. A heavy male voice answered.

"This is Jack Stuart."

"Jack, this is Michael Smith at Metro Cablevision. How is everything going?"

"Mike! Everything is going well. It is good to hear your voice. How are you doing?"

"Never better," Smith said. "I have a situation that I need your help on."

"Sure thing," replied Stuart. "What do you need?"

"We've had a series of vehicle break-ins, and I'd like to try again to get management onboard with the Cyber-Trace software. But what I need from you is a complete sales presentation package."

"That shouldn't be a problem. There is a regional sales representative in your area that I will place you in contact with. It should not be too difficult to convince your management team to use the product. Metro is already a corporate subscriber."

"Is that right? Well, that's great news. Have your rep give me a call, and we will work out the details."

"Sure thing," said Stuart. "Is there anything else I can help you with?"

"Not at the moment, but I'll call you and let you know if there is."

"Thank you, Mike, and thank you for calling."

"Talk with you soon, Jack."

He hung up the phone and rubbed his chin.

"That should just about do it," he said, rising from his seat.

He turned off the computer, placed his phone on "Do Not Disturb," and walked out of the office, turning off the lights and locking the door behind him.

"Tomorrow is another day."

CHAPTER FIVE

Just Another Day

Smith did not want to work late, so he went in an hour early. It was early Thursday morning, and the parking lot was still partially empty. He found a space quickly, parked and gathered his files and notebook.

"It's going to be a good day," he thought, as he emerged from the vehicle.

Smith and his son went to karate practice on Tuesday and Thursday nights. They had already missed the Tuesday night class and could not afford to miss another lesson. Their drive to the studio took over forty-five minutes in the late afternoon traffic. The class started promptly at 7:15 PM, and Smith refused to arrive late. He did not like to anger Master Chang, but also, he needed the extra time to warm up and stretch before class.

Michael Jr. was already a first-degree black

belt. He started taking karate at the age of five. By the time he was twelve years old, he was ready to test for his *Cho Dan*.

Smith never forced his son to stay in karate or continue his training, but he often suggested how useful it would be later in life. Michael Jr. enjoyed the time he spent with his dad in training, and always demonstrated a high degree of respect and self-discipline.

As a youngster Smith studied *Shotokan* and *Ch'uan Fa Kempo* and understood the value of discipline and self-respect. Now well into his 50's, he was once again on a disciple's journey, traveling the path of *Soo Bahk Do*.

In his own Cho Dan candidate essay, "What Does Soo Bahk Do Mean to Me?", Smith had written:

> Soo Bahk Do is a way of life.
>
> I began training under David Chang, Sa Bom Nim in September 1999. I knew at that time it would be tough getting back into shape after being dormant for over 20 years. As a young man in Chicago, I studied Shotokan karate under Sensei Thomas Jordan from 1968 to 1969. I attained the

rank of Green Belt before enlisting into the United States Air Force to fulfill my military obligation.

After my tour of duty, I moved to Compton, California, where I studied for a time under Sensei Brandon Childs. My training over the next few years was sporadic and included different styles of martial arts like Ch'uan Fa Kempo. This trend continued until September 1977.

And as fate would have it, after reaching a plateau of proficiency, my direction was diverted toward mundane activities. Eventually, I lost most of what I had studied and trained so hard to attain. And though I remained physically active, I did not continue my martial arts training. Instead, I turned my attention toward career, higher education, and eventually, home and family.

And yet as the body of the dragon physically wasted away, the spirit of the art, the heart of the dragon, remained intact. For twenty years, the dragon slept undisturbed.

Then, in September 1997, my five-year-old son brought a flier home from school. It was a promotional ad from a local karate studio offering martial arts training to children. My wife and I agreed that it would be a good investment in our son's future, and we enrolled him into the David Chang Martial Arts Academy under the guidance of Kyo Sa Nim, David Chang.

Mr. Chang, as we were instructed to call him at that time, was a dedicated young man with a passion for the martial art he was teaching. That passion was infectious and inspiring, and soon, the Do Jang had become our home away from home.

As my son tested and received promotions, I eagerly purchased the training manuals. That way, I was able to help him with his forms, terminology, and one-step sparring. For me it was a wonderful experience, and I was growing vicariously through him. But something was missing, and my son sensed it.

One day after class he asked me to join martial arts with him. There were several parents in the Do Jang, who were already training with their children. My son wanted to experience that oneness as well. I thought about it for a few moments, and then I made him a promise. I said, "When you reach the rank of Green Belt, I will begin taking Soo Bahk Do." True to my word, I began training in September 1999.

Soo Bahk Do is discipline, loyalty, and faithfulness.

There were many days when work hampered my ability to professionally train. We moved to Oceanside, and I began taking computer networking courses at the local community college. There were weeks of scheduling conflicts when classroom study and homework assignments took their toll in both time and energy and pushed me farther away from training in the Do Jang. There were months when physical injury prevented me from continuing and advancing in rank. I had reached a plateau and could not move forward. There were bumps and roadblocks on my path.

One could say these were simply excuses, and it would not be totally untrue. A martial arts practitioner must learn to overcome adversity, regardless of the form it takes. But these were obstacles that I allowed to control and change my course. I became lax and unfocused. Eventually, this took its toll in an unexpected way. I noticed that my son had lost his joy and enthusiasm for training in Soo Bahk Do. That was unacceptable.

I found the courage to overcome the challenges and take back control of my life. My son's spirit was revived and his eagerness to learn returned. I watched as his techniques, focus and concentration improved by leaps and bounds. We were both back on track.

By the time my son was promoted to the rank of first GUP and had become a candidate for Cho Dan, I was determined to keep his training consistent. We trained with Leo Baxter, Sa Bom Nim on Sunday afternoons, but we remained faithful to David Chang, Sa Bom Nim, attending all required classes during the week, as well as the special candidate classes on Saturday mornings. We were dedicated and determined. My son was promoted to Cho Dan. And now it is my turn. I have begun my own Cho Dan training, and I am determined to finish what I have begun.

Soo Bahk Do is the union and oneness of mind, body, and spirit.

It is not a sport. It is a classical martial art that helps to develop a person that is free of inner conflict and can deal with the outer world in a calm, intellectual and mature manner. The three areas of human development in Soo Bahk Do (Shim Gung, Neh Gung and Weh Gung) integrate the intellect, body, emotions, and spirit.

Learning the principles and philosophy of Soo Bahk Do has helped me in both my personal and professional life. It has aided me in developing inner strength, and a calm, poised exterior. I have learned to face conflict with quiet resolve, and to allow the natural flow of events to occur.

As I recall my early days of training as a young man, I realize that I did not have the correct focus or discipline to be a true martial artist. Indeed, I practiced karate, but I did not understand the connection between the art and the world around me. Shotokan helped me to gain confidence in my physical ability to defend myself, but there was no connection with justice or honor. Kempo taught me how to destroy an opponent, but it did not teach me how to connect with my fellow man.

Soo Bahk Do has filled the void, that emptiness which separates the artist from his art. The moment I saw Soo Bahk Do in practice; I knew it was the martial art I had been seeking. Yet, it took the courage of a five-year-old child, innocently sharing the flier he had brought home from school, to remind me of that which I had long since forgotten.

"I am the art, and the art is always within me. We are one and the same."

The dragon has been awakened!

Soo Bahk!!!

Smith appreciated the time he spent with his son and often told him how proud he was of him. Michael Jr. dreamed of becoming a fighter pilot. He enjoyed playing video games and often coaxed his dad into taking a turn with the game controller. Smith was not exceptionally good at video gaming but did occasionally enjoy playing Donkey Kong on an old Nintendo 64. Michael Jr.

played all the cool games on Xbox.

"Dad, are we going to karate tonight?" Michael Jr. had asked earlier while he prepared for school.

"I sure hope so," Smith had responded. "That is why I am going into work early, so we'll have enough time to get through all the traffic. You know how I hate to be late for class."

"Yeah, cool. Well, we have missed a lot of classes and you need the practice. You'll be testing for your black belt in less than two weeks."

It was true. Smith did need more practice. And though the Dan Shim Sa was just days away, there were still areas of training he needed to improve. But in all, the martial arts helped Smith to overcome stress, and outwardly, he projected an air of *peaceful confidence*. This aided him immensely in his interaction with people, both socially and professionally.

"Yes," he whispered softly, "this is going to be a good day."

Smith walked past the security guard as he entered the building.

"Good morning Janice."

"Good morning," replied the uniformed officer. "Well, today will be my last day with you folks. The new company will be taking over, and I'm being transferred to another site."

"Sorry to see you go," Smith said, trying to sound earnest.

He knew the real reason Janice was being let go. There had been a conflict between her and another guard, a miscommunication where a statement she had made caused some embarrassment for the company. They still held it against her, and now they were using this opportunity to get rid of her. It was not common knowledge. But still, Janice was dependable and trustworthy.

The Metro employees in the building did not particularly care for the other guard. He bragged a lot, and often exceeded his authority. In Smith's opinion, keeping him and letting Janice go was just another bad business decision.

"Not my problem," he thought, as he opened the door to his office.

He entered, put his keys into the desk drawer and turned on his computer. The hard drive screeched as the machine came to life. He typed in his username and password, logged onto the network, and waited for the servers to connect. He turned his head and noticed that the light on the telephone was blinking, indicating there was a voicemail message. He punched in his code on the keypad and listened to the message.

"Hi Mike. My name is Josh Miller. I am a detective with the Oceanside PD. I am trying to confirm whether you guys provide service to a certain telephone number. According to an Internet search which I did, Metro comes up. But I just need to verify that. I am writing a search warrant for this number, but if you could verify for me, I'd greatly appreciate it. The number is 760-295-5555, and my contact number, desk number, is 760-435-5555. Thanks a lot."

Smith replayed the message several times, capturing bits of information with each pass. When he collected all the pertinent data, he reached for his computer mouse and clicked the icon that opened a window to the customer database. He entered the telephone number into the search field, hit the enter key and waited. A window popped up with the customer record. He read the activity screen and realized the customer's account had been disconnected the previous day.

Smith did not speculate. He picked up the phone and called the detective… voicemail. He left a message.

"Detective Miller, this is Michael Smith at Metro Cablevision returning your call. With regards to the telephone number, you were inquiring about, that is affirmative. Your Internet search was correct. The number is in our database. If you have any questions, give me a call. Thanks."

Smith kept the message short and vague on purpose. He was extremely careful not to divulge subscriber information without the proper authorization. That fact that the detective had already conducted an Internet search and came up with Metro Cablevision as the service provider placed the exchange in the *gray area.*

He turned back toward his computer and opened a new daily activity log. It was routine.

He checked his email messages, and then started his daily log. The telephone rang.

"Metro Cablevision, Network Security; this is Michael Smith. I can help you."

"Hey Mike. It is Josh Miller at OPD. I got your message. Thanks."

"No problem. What can I help you with?"

"I have another number that I need to verify."

"Sure. What's the number?"

Miller gave him the number. Smith typed it into the search field and conducted another database search. The account was active.

"That is affirmative, Josh. It's one of ours."

"Great. Thanks Mike I really appreciate your assistance."

"No problem. You be safe out there."

"Thanks, and you do the same."

Smith hung up the phone and returned to the activity log. He typed a few lines, and then picked up a violation report that was sitting on his desk. He read it.

"Okay, this needs to be worked today," he said to himself, and he started typing an incident supplementary. He opened a file folder and downloaded several photographs into the document.

The violation report stated the account had not been active since 2002. During a routine street inspection, the cable line was found to be connected. The inspector disconnected the cable wire and placed a red warning label on the line. He then went back a month later to recheck the line and found it had been illegally reconnected again. The inspector stated in the report that the cable fitting was finger-tight, indicating that whoever connected it did not use the proper tools. He had taken several photographs, emailed them and turned the entire case over to Smith for investigation and door contact.

Smith completed the document and gathered his notebook. He clipped a field investigation packet to the violation report and attached the supplemental document. He turned off the lights, locked the office door behind him and walked out of the building.

It was a bright autumn day, and the air was

warm. Smith opened the car door and placed his notebook inside. He slowly climbed into the driver's seat and started the engine. Mentally rehearsing the door contact approach, he visualized the interior of the suspect's home. He contemplated what lay beyond the front door, in rooms where televisions connected to cable service. In his mind he imagined a mishmash of furniture scattered throughout the living room, a television in an entertainment center, videotapes, and a VCR. The images melted one into the other until they were a blur, and all the rooms in the house looked the same. He focused on the cable wires that were connected to the televisions. The images became clearer. He could now see the suspect, resisting, challenging, and not at all cooperative. He cleared his mind and placed the vehicle into reverse. Slowly he exited from the parking space, placed the car into drive and pulled out onto the street. He breathed easily.

"It's just another day," he thought, "...same as always."

CHAPTER SIX
Field of Vision

Smith drove slowly past the house. He could see that someone was home. The front door was open. He pulled around the corner, parked on the adjacent street and made the call.

"Oceanside Police Department, this is Dispatcher 21. How can I help you?"

"Hi, my name is Michael Smith. I am an investigator with Metro Cablevision, and I am in the process of contacting some people whom we suspect are stealing our cable television services. I'd like to have an officer standby and preserve the peace while I conduct the investigation."

"Are you at the location now?"

"Yes ma'am, I right around the corner from the suspect's residence."

"What is the address that you are going to?"

"The address is 605 Cora Street."

"Is there an apartment number?"

"No ma'am, it's a single-family dwelling."

"Are you calling from a cell phone?"

"Yes ma'am."

"What's the number?"

"It's area code 619, 977-5555."

"And are you in a cable truck?"

"No ma'am, I'm in a red unmarked Chevy Blazer."

"And where would you like for the officers to meet you?"

"I'm at the corner of Cora and Silver Street."

"Okay, I sent a unit out as soon as one is available."

"Thank you, ma'am," Smith stated, "and have a good day."

"You're welcome," said the dispatcher.

Smith expected to wait for at least a half

hour. He opened a brown paper bag that was sitting on the seat and took out an apple. It was red and juicy. He took a bite and savored the flavor. A moment later, a police unit pulled up next to him.

Smith scurried out of the vehicle and walked over to the cruiser.

"Wow, that was quick," Smith said.

"I was right up the street when the call went out."

"My name is Michael Smith. I'm an investigator for Metro Cablevision."

"I'm Officer Landau, and I think we've met," said the policeman. "It's been a while, but I did one of these investigations with you. It was an apartment building downtown. The resident wasn't home, and you ended up just turning off the cable."

"I think I remember. It has been a while. Well, today there is someone at home. The front door is open and there's activity inside. Are you expecting a cover unit, or are we going to do this by ourselves?"

"We can do it ourselves," replied Landau.

Smith hesitated for a moment, as a thought flashed through his mind.

"Do you know anything about this address or the occupants?" he asked the officer.

"No, but I can check and see if there's any history. Let me call my supervisor and see how he wants me to handle this."

The officer made a call on his cell phone, as another unit approached.

"Backup unit," thought Smith. "That's good."

Having an officer standing by to preserve the peace while he conducted his investigation was how Smith liked it; but having two policemen present was even better. Landau finished the call and walked toward Smith.

"We're good to go," he said.

The second officer emerged from his cruiser. Officer Landau approached him.

"This is the investigator for Metro Cablevision," Landau stated. "There's someone stealing the cable television service. Have you ever done one of these?"

"No. This is the first," said Officer Dean Hofstadter.

"Basically, this will be a knock and talk. If we get inside the investigator will check to see if the cable is being used. If it is then he will make a citizen's arrest and we'll issue a citation."

Landau turned toward Smith.

"How successful are you at getting into the residence?"

"For the most part, pretty successful," he responded. "There have been times when we've been told to go pound sand, but mostly, we get inside."

"What if they don't let us in?"

"If the television is in my *field of vision*, and I can determine that it is receiving cable services, then I may ask them to step *outside*. If they do, I'll place them under arrest then."

"How successful are you at getting your cases prosecuted by the DA?" Landau asked.

"Very successful," Smith responded. "My case narrative is as about as complete as it could possibly be with synopsis, background, suspects' statements and photographs."

"Okay, then let's do it."

The three men walked toward the suspect's house. It was around the corner, second from the end. As they approached, they observed a man was outside in the driveway. He appeared to be working.

"Afternoon, sir," said Smith. "Are you the resident here?"

"No," the man responded, "but my friend is. There's someone inside."

"What's the name of the residents?" Smith inquired.

"Jackson," he replied.

"And what's their first name?"

"Kathleen," he responded.

"Thanks," Smith said as he walked toward the door, the policemen just a few steps behind. He paused at the entrance. There was a screen door obscuring his field of vision into the residence, even though the main door was open. He could barely make out the silhouette of someone moving about inside.

"Hello," Smith shouted.

"Yes, can I help you?" replied a female voice inside.

"Ms. Jackson?" Smith said politely.

"Yes," she acknowledged as she opened the screen door. Kathleen Jackson was a housewife and mother in her mid to late thirties. Her hair was pulled back into a ponytail. Dressed in a plain shirt and jeans, she appeared to have been doing housework when the men arrived. Smith introduced himself.

"Ms. Jackson, my name is Michael Smith. I am an investigator with Metro Cablevision," he said, as he presented his photo identification. He turned and gestured toward the policemen standing behind him. "These officers are here as a precaution for my safety and to preserve the peace. The reason I am here today is because of the cable television service that you have. I would like to come in and speak with you about it."

"Okay," she said, "but we don't have cable service here." She opened to door wide enough for the men to enter.

Smith noticed the television off to his left as he entered the house. It was sitting in an entertainment center and appeared to be attached to a VCR. He could not tell if it was connected to the cable service.

"May I inspect the television and the connections?" he asked.

"Sure," she replied, "but we don't have any cable service here. And the television doesn't work."

"I'd like to take a look," Smith said.

A young man entered the living room. He was husky a teenager and appeared to be about sixteen years old.

"What the hell is this?" he inquired in a hostile tone. "Is this a goddamn crime or something?"

The officers did not respond. Smith kept his attention focused on the television and the cable connections in the back.

"Sam, stop it," his mother shouted. The boy's anger was apparent. He hated authority figures.

"Why are they here?" he asked in the same hostile voice.

"It's not your concern," she replied. "Just go outside or go to your room. But don't say anything else."

The young man complied and walked out of the room. Smith glanced at the officers. They were both shaking their heads, apparently thinking the same thing.

"How do you turn on the TV?" Smith asked the woman.

"It doesn't work," she said.

"Are there any other televisions in the house?" he asked.

"Yes," she said hesitantly.

Smith waited for her to move. She turned slowly and walked toward the bedrooms. She stopped at a door and tried to turn the knob. It was locked.

"Whose room is that?" Smith asked.

"That's my oldest son's room," she answered. "He's away on a JROTC event."

"Is he off at Coronado?" Smith asked.

"No, it's Junior ROTC."

"There is a high school ROTC event on Coronado Island," Smith said. "Is he participating in that event?"

"Oh, I don't know," she admitted, and went on to say that her son was a senior at El Camino High School.

Smith concealed his reaction, smiled, and nodded, as she turned and walked into another bedroom. There was a small TV/VCR combo unit sitting on top of the dresser. It appeared to be connected to a cable wire. Smith asked her to turn the set on.

"We really don't have any cable service here," Ms. Jackson said again. "I've been watching a videotape."

Smith did not respond. She turned on the television. A clear picture appeared on the screen with the USA Network logo in the lower right-hand corner. The set was tuned to Channel 35.

"Oh, I see we do have cable service," she

said, trying hard to sound surprised. "So, can we watch it?"

Again, Smith said nothing. He jotted down some comments in his notebook.

"So," he said finally, "I see the cable service is working. Whose room is this?"

"It's my room," she responded. "It's mine and my husband's."

"How did the cable service get turned on?" he asked in a monotone voice.

"I don't know anything about the cable service being on," she insisted. "You'll have to talk to my husband about that."

At that moment Henry Jackson walked into the house. A tall, slender man, he wore large wire-rimmed glasses. Smith approached him and presented his photo identification.

"Mr. Jackson, my name is Michael Smith. I am an investigator with Metro Cablevision. As I explained to your wife before I entered the residence, the officers are here as a precaution for my safety and to preserve the peace."

Jackson appeared calm and undisturbed by

the presence of the two uniformed policemen in his house.

"Like I indicated to your wife before you arrived, I am here to investigate the unauthorized cable service that you are receiving. How long have you lived here, sir?"

"About fourteen years," he responded.

Smith opened his notebook. He flipped through the pages of his investigation packet and stopped on the field incident document. There were several photographs, which depicted the illegal cable connection at the underground equipment outside the residence. Smith pointed to one of the photographs.

"As you can see, the cable box outside has been damaged and can no longer be secured. Your cable wire was disconnected by one of our technicians about one month ago. Now it is back on. How do you explain that?"

Jackson hesitated, thinking about his response. Smith did not waste time. He closed the notebook.

"Come with me," he insisted. "I want you to see the television in the master bedroom."

Jackson followed Smith without speaking.

"Please turn on the television," Smith requested politely.

Jackson picked up the remote control and turned on the television. A bright clear picture appeared on the screen. The USA Network logo was prominently displayed in the lower right-hand corner. Jackson handed the controller to Smith.

"When we first arrived," Smith continued, "your wife told me there was no cable service in the house. But when she turned the television on, there was the USA Network. The TV was tuned to Channel 35, which clearly demonstrates that someone was using the cable service."

Smith switched to another channel. Again, a bright clear picture appeared on the screen. He continued this through the entire channel lineup. Jackson was receiving all tiers of the basic cable service.

"Now can you tell me how the cable service got reconnected?"

"We happened to mention to someone that

we didn't have cable service and they had it hooked up."

"Who would that have been?" Smith asked.

"A family acquaintance named Bob Gordon. He died a couple of months ago. But he lived here occasionally, and while he was here, he noticed that we did not have cable service. So, he told us he would take care of it."

"And so, this person hooked up the cable service for you?"

"Either he did, or he had someone to do it for him."

"And how long ago was that?" Smith asked.

"About a year ago," Jackson replied.

"Now you say that Bob Gordon died a couple of months ago," Smith continued, "but the line was disconnected one month ago. Who connected the line after it had been disconnected recently?"

"To be honest, I don't know."

Smith continued asking questions designed to establish willful knowledge of the crime that had been committed. He read a section of the Penal Code which applied to the case and asked Jackson if he understood.

Jackson said, "I understand."

Then Smith asked him for his identification and was handed a driver's license. He continued asking questions, gathering personal information that he needed to complete the report.

Finally, Smith asked, "Did you think it was wrong, or even illegal to use the cable service without paying for it?"

Jackson responded, "Both wrong and illegal."

Smith then asked Jackson to review and sign the questionnaires, to verify that his responses had been recorded correctly. After doing so, Smith photographed him and finished the interview in his usual manner.

"Sir, I'm placing you under citizen's arrest for violation of California Penal Code 593d (a) (1), the unauthorized use of cable television services. The officer will issue you a citation and explain the process."

Smith handed the driver's license to Officer

Landau, who issued the citation.

"You understand, sir," began Landau, "that by signing this ticket, you are promising to appear on the date and at the time specified. You may or may not receive a notice in the mail confirming this date. But in case you do not receive a notification from the court, you still need to show up on this date. Do you understand?"

"I understand," replied Jackson.

"Do you have any questions?" Landau asked.

"No, I don't," he said.

Smith stood in the doorway and waited for the officer to finish before he spoke.

"Mr. Jackson, do you have any questions for me?"

"I did, but I can't remember just this minute. If you want to leave a business card, I could call you when I remember; or maybe not."

Smith thought about it, recalling the fact that Jackson's eldest son was a senior and attended the same high school as Michael Jr.

Both were in ROTC, and he imagined they probably knew each other. He did not want to create a hostile situation for his son.

"No, I do not," Smith responded. "Any questions you have you need to ask me now."

Jackson dropped his head and said, "I can't think of anything right now."

Smith turned and walked out the door. He told the officers that he would disconnect the illegal cable line, and then return to his office to complete the case narrative. Later that day, Smith hand delivered his report to Landau.

CHAPTER SEVEN
A Tangled Web

Smith got out of bed a little later than normal. He was going to court on one of his cable-theft cases. The person he had arrested was an older woman. He recalled the incident clearly.

It was exactly two months ago that he arrived at Charlotte Casey's apartment. He knocked, the door swung open and a young man around the age of twenty-two was standing there looking Smith squarely in the eyes. He was about six feet tall with dark brown shoulder length hair, and a small goatee; he wore a blue baseball cap, white tee shirt and faded jeans.

"Yeah, can I help you?" he asked.

"Are you the resident here?" Smith inquired.

At that moment, the young man noticed the police officer standing to the left of Smith.

Startled, he reacted in a very suspicious manner.

"No, I'm not," he replied, as he began to close the door.

The police officer who accompanied Smith moved quickly, inserting his boot against the door to prevent it from closing.

"Don't you dare close that door in my face," Officer Brian Hughes admonished.

He pushed the door open and entered the apartment. The young man's actions triggered a violent response, causing Hughes to react aggressively. Smith stood by, while the officer assessed the situation inside. Hughes was there to preserve the peace, and he wanted to be sure the site was safe and secure.

With the door wide open and his view unobstructed, Smith saw there were two young women in the living room with the young man. They were both seated on the sofa. From the expression on their faces, it was apparent they had been engaging in some illegal activity. They were obviously trying to hide something. For a moment Smith thought he detected a faint smell of marijuana in the air. He ignored it. That was not the reason for his visit. Later however, he would discover the real reason behind their suspicious behavior.

Smith sat at his breakfast table sipping a cup of hot herbal tea. The quiet of the morning was consoling. He visualized himself dressed in his navy-blue pin striped suit with a royal blue shirt and matching floral tie. That would be his attire.

The District Attorney had filed and issued the case against Casey, and today was the arraignment. She would either plead guilty or not guilty. Smith would be there to assist the deputy DA with any questions regarding restitution if the issue arose.

He finished his tea and pushed away from the table. He placed the cup into the sink and rinsed it with clear water.

"Don't forget the case file," he thought. "I can't go to court without the case."

Smith stripped off his pajamas and turned on the shower. He waited for a few minutes, and then stepped inside. The warm water was refreshing, as the stream splashed against his face and soaked his hair. It was relaxing. The soothing moisture helped clear his mind, allowing him to think more clearly.

He recalled the investigation and the sequence of events leading to the arrest. The tension in his muscles dissipated as the water massaged his body.

Charlotte Casey had been resting in her bedroom the day Smith arrived to arrest her for cable TV theft. The three young people in her apartment were just visitors.

"Where is the resident?" Smith asked once he was confident the area was secured.

"It's my adopted mother," answered one of the young women. "She's in the bedroom. I will get her. Can you tell me what this is all about?"

"I'd rather speak with the resident," Smith said.

The girl, who later identified herself as Sarah, went into the bedroom. A few minutes later she returned.

"She'll be right out," announced Sarah.

Smith waited. Casey emerged from the bedroom wearing a bathrobe. She appeared disheveled, as though she had just been awakened from a very deep sleep.

"What's going on?" she asked the officer.

"This is the cable TV investigator," he said pointing to Smith. "He's here to talk to you about the cable service you're getting for free."

"I don't know anything about any cable service," she said reaching for a pack of cigarettes.

Smith was still standing outside. He presented his photo identification and explained why he was there. He told Casey that the officer was present as a precaution of safety and to preserve the peace while he conducted this investigation for Metro Cablevision. He then asked for permission to enter her residence, and she invited him inside.

The young man, who had identified himself as Josh, breathed a sigh of relief and smirked.

"So, this is just about the cable TV?" he asked.

"That's correct," Smith replied.

"Then in that case, can we go?" Josh asked.

"Sure, there's no reason you need to stay,"

said Hughes.

The three young people gathered their belongings and proceeded to leave as Smith began his interview. Casey lit a cigarette and noxious fumes filled the air.

"Do you mind if I check the television?" Smith asked.

"Go ahead," Casey responded.

The 27" color TV sitting in the entertainment center was turned off. Smith inspected the wires behind the set and saw that it was connected to the line coming from a cable television outlet.

"Can you please turn on the television?" he asked.

Casey picked up the remote control and powered up the television. A fuzzy, but viewable picture appeared on the screen. The TV was tuned to Channel 34-TNT. After Smith had verified the set was receiving all tiers of basic service, he asked if there were any other televisions in the residence. Casey told him there was a TV in the bedroom. He asked her to show him.

"The bedroom is kind of messy, and my friend is asleep in there," she said.

"That's not a problem," insisted Smith. "I've seen just about every situation you can imagine."

Casey led the way to the bedroom. A man in his late forties, who identified himself as Vance Fontaine, was lying in bed watching the History Channel on a 19" color TV.

"I'm disabled," Fontaine said. "I hope you don't mind if I don't get up."

Smith assured him it was okay, and that he would not take long with his inspection. He verified the TV was receiving all tiers of basic cable service, while Casey watched him navigate through the channels.

"How did the cable get hooked up?" he asked.

"I don't know," Casey responded, lighting another cigarette.

"A friend of a friend came by and hooked up the cable," Fontaine blurted out, sitting up in bed.

Smith could not figure out if Fontaine thought he was helping Casey by divulging that information, or if he were really trying to make sure she got arrested.

"Who was the friend?" Smith asked.

Casey shuffled and took a drag off her cigarette. Then she stated, "A girlfriend named Rita came over with her boyfriend and he hooked it up."

"Who do you think reconnected the cable service outside?"

"One of the old maintenance guys," she said.

Casey admitted that she knew the cable service was on illegally, and that she was committing a crime. Smith gave her a copy of the California Penal Code 593d and read the section of the law that pertained to her case. He then placed her under citizen's arrest, and Officer Hughes issued the citation.

Smith turned off the shower and reached for his towel. Twenty minutes later he was dressed and ready to go. He got into the red Chevy Blazer, opened the garage door with the remote, and started the engine.

The drive to the courthouse took less than half an hour. He arrived at 8:45 AM. The bailiff greeted him as he entered the courtroom.

"Good morning," Deputy Kidd said with a smile. "We haven't seen you here for a while."

"Trying to keep low key," Smith replied. "You know how it is."

Smith knew how important it was to maintain a good rapport with law enforcement and the District Attorney's office. He went out of his way to keep from stepping on anyone's toes. He was always cordial and polite to everyone he met, including the crusty (sometimes sleazy) defense attorneys who frequented the halls of justice, trolling for new scumbags to defend.

The courtroom was filled with defendants, co-defendants, and personal friends of defendants. Most were there for health and safety code violations, drunken driving, and petty theft. Misdemeanor arraignment court was the first stop for many of them. Some would plead guilty or no contest, while others would swear, they were innocent and demand a jury trial and court-appointed attorney. Of those who plead not guilty, a good percentage would plead out at the readiness hearing, or shortly before going to trial.

Smith was familiar with the court process. Ninety per cent of the cases he submitted to the DA were issued for prosecution. Eighty-five per cent of those pled out and paid restitution to the company. Most received three years informal probation, a modest fine to the court, and some were required to perform community service work. A few were hit with 4th Amendment waivers.

Smith was almost certain Casey would plead not guilty and demand a jury trial. He had seen enough defendants in similar situations try to bargain their way out of huge fines or jail time by pushing back against the DA; hoping the stall tactics would force a better deal than they would get if they pled guilty at the arraignment. He scanned the court room for the familiar face of the woman he had arrested. She was there, sitting amongst the crowd, awaiting her turn to speak with the public defender. Smith noticed that she did not seem as haggard as she had been on the day, he arrested her; the day she discovered that stealing cable television services was more serious than people realized. The fact is, she appeared illuminated, smiling, as if she had won the lottery. She was nicely dressed and wore a modest amount of makeup. Smith was impressed. He thought back to the day when he and Officer Hughes first contacted her.

After the arrest Smith and Hughes exited the apartment. They were starting the paperwork on the citizen's arrest when Hughes received a radio call from the police dispatcher.

"There is a vice detective in your area," she advised "that needs to speak with you regarding the address you are at."

"We're not in the apartment anymore," Hughes responded. "We've finished with the investigation."

"Standby, the detective is on his way."

"That's 10-4…standing by."

The radio went silent. A few moments later, a plainly dressed, middle-aged man approached them. He was somewhat pudgy but walked quickly as with a definite purpose and objective. Hughes recognized the man as Mike

Stark, a detective on the vice squad.

"When I heard you were at this address I rushed right over," Stark said, breathing heavily, as though he had just run a marathon. "We've had our eye on this location for some time. There is a parolee at large, a punk kid by the name of Josh Pratt that hangs out here with his girlfriend, Sarah. He's wanted in connection with a series of vehicle burglaries and grand theft auto."

Hughes looked at Smith and they both realized what had occurred. They had been inches away from Pratt in Casey's apartment. Then it all made sense. When Smith and Hughes arrived at the apartment, Pratt thought they were there to arrest him. That was the reason for his suspicious behavior. But when he discovered that it was a cable TV investigation (and he was not the target), he breathed a sigh of relief and smirked; picked up his backpack and took off.

"He was in the apartment," Hughes said. "He was right there, and we let him get away."

Just as Smith had predicted, Casey pled not guilty and requested a trial by jury. He left the courtroom feeling empty inside.

A few months later he received a call from the DA's office informing him that the charges against Casey had been bumped up to a felony. *Casey* was apparently an alias for *Charlotte Walters*, previously convicted on theft charges with a prison prior. It looked as though she was going *back* to jail. The DA, however, dismissed the felony charges, and she was convicted of cable theft. She was placed on three years' probation and ordered to perform 40 hours of community service work. But Casey (a.k.a. Walters) never showed up to enroll in the work program. Her probation was revoked; she was eventually picked up and sent to jail.

Smith closed the case file, reminiscing on the elements of the investigation and its ultimate outcome. He smiled, thinking,

"Such a tangled web she weaves."

CHAPTER EIGHT

An Undercover Sting Operation

On August 19, 1996, when he received the first flyer from employee Stuart Gillian, advertising illegally modified cable boxes, Smith knew the only way to catch the thief would be in an undercover sting operation. And that would require upper management authorization. Smith would need a strong justification and a solid plan and solution for carrying out the sting operation. He would secure site that would be easy for the suspect to connect the cable service. He would also need up-front money to make the first purchase. And later, he would need additional cash to make the real "big" purchase. That would take time, but he needed more than a single flyer to get started. Smith placed the flyer inside a folder and dropped it with the *pending cases* file.

Over the next several months, he received several more reports of flyers being distributed throughout the county, offering unlimited access to all cable television premium and pay-per-view services. Then, on February 7, 1997 while conducting a separate theft of service investigation, Smith was given a Penny Saver ad. The suspect in that case, Marianne Schneider, admitted responding to the ad. She said a man who called himself William Metro came out and connected the cable service. He installed a cable box that decoded all the premium and pay-per-view channels. She said she paid $150 for the box. Armed with this information and the stack of reports, Smith approached his boss, Simon Butcher.

"Simon, I need to talk to you about an important case that I'm working on."

"Okay."

Butcher appeared detached, distracted. His workload doubled after Corporate decided to consolidate all Southern California into one system. He was responsible for the physical security of *all* facilities and assets in the region, in addition to resolving the theft of service cases.

"We have received numerous reports of some guy distributing flyers around the county, offering modified decoders and free cable TV service. This one is going to require a *sting operation*."

"Tell me what you need, and I will run it up the chain."

Smith recorded a full account of the sting operation in his Case narrative:

> On August 19th, 1996, I received an advertisement flier from Metro Cablevision employee, Stuart Gillian. The flier was promoting the sale of cable television converters and descramblers. According to Gillian, he discovered the flier, which was left on the windshield of his car, shortly after midnight on August 12th, 1996. His vehicle had been parked in the Wells Fargo Bank parking lot, located at 510 W. Washington Street, San Diego, 92103. The telephone number, listed on the flier, was (619) 620-5555. I called the number, which was connected to an answering machine. I did not leave a message.
>
> On August 21st, 1996, I received another flier bearing the same telephone number, (619) 620-5555; however, the

new flier contained the name Cable Box Suppliers, Inc. I called Operator Information, and asked for the telephone number to Cable Box Suppliers, Inc. I was told there was no listing for any company by that name. Other ads were forwarded to System Security with the same, or similar information.

On February 7th, 1997, during another theft of service investigation, the suspect indicated that she knew of a person named William Metro, who advertises the sale of cable descramblers. The suspect, Marianne Schneider, CCSD Case# 96-09-753, produced a telephone number from her rolodex. The name William Metro was written at the top with the number 620-5555.

On February 12th, 1997, I contacted San Diego Police Det. Paul Rutledge, and informed him of the pending investigation. Det. Rutledge gave me permission to surreptitiously record all phone conversations with the suspect(s). At approximately 1408 hours (2:08 PM), I placed a call to 620-5555. The phone was connected to an answering machine, and the greeting message indicated that I had reached Nu-Tek Electronics. I left the name Victor Anderson, and my "burner cell phone" number, 887-0254. At approximately 1535 hours (3:35 PM), I received a return call. The caller identified himself as Bill. He stated that he had Pioneer decoders available for $250 each, which were guaranteed to descramble all the premium and pay-per-view channels. I asked if there would be a discount if I purchased 5 or more boxes. He said that if I purchased all five at the same time, he would sell them to me for $200 per unit. I told him that I would call him back when I was ready to purchase a cable box. He gave me another number to contact him, 620-5555. The conversation was recorded.

The narrative continued:

On February 25th, 1997, at approximately 1145hours, the suspect arrived at my studio apartment, located at 5090 El Cajon Blvd. Unit 31, 92105. He was not carrying the decoder with him. Upon entering the unit, the suspect asked me a series of questions (e.g., "Are you a police officer, or work for the cable company?"

and "What do you do?"). He then proceeded to inspect the cable attachment to the television. I indicated that the hotel cable service included HBO, but none of the pay-per-view channels. I showed him that I had the $250.00 for the cable box, and some additional money which I had collected from a couple of other people. I told him that I would soon have the rest of the up-front cash for the additional five decoders at $200.00 each. He said that he only had the one box with him and would get it from his car. He returned to his vehicle, which he had parked on the south side of El Cajon Blvd., in the parking lot behind the Max 99 Cents discount store. A few minutes later, he came back to the apartment carrying a plastic grocery bag.

The suspect proceeded to connect the cable box to the television. He verified that it was receiving all Premium and pay-per-view channels. He asked if I wanted to buy a universal remote control for an additional $10.00, and I told him that I had not budgeted for it but might consider buying one in the future. The suspect offered to sell me two boxes for $200.00

each, saying that he would do so, because he was sure that I would be buying more later. He told me that he buys the boxes from a local technician, who modifies the boxes and sells them wholesale for $150.00 each. He went on to say that the technician buys the "raw" boxes for $40.00 - $50.00 each and adds a program chip which costs about $10.00. He stated that he would pay me $20.00 for each "raw" unreturned decoder that I found or got hold of.

He told me the modified box was guaranteed, and showed me the initials R.L.J., which had been written on the bottom of the box in a black marker. He said that those were the initials of the technician who modified the box. This was to indicate that the box was under a six-month warranty, and that the technician could identify the decoder as one which he had modified.

He told me that he also sells the two-piece converter-descrambler units for about $130.00 each, and that he purchases these through mail order. He stated that most customers prefer the single unit because there is less to hook up. The suspect said that he would like for me to see the two-piece unit. He indicated that, for the moment, he has a steady supply of decoders, but when he cannot get them, he sells the converter-descrambler units.

I told the suspect that I would get in contact with him very soon to purchase the additional decoders. He then left the apartment but did not immediately leave the area. Instead, he went to the discount store across the street and purchased some items. Once he departed the area, one of the SDPD detective units followed him home. They ran the vehicle plate number, and found that the car was registered to William Barton, who resides at 4319 Copperfield Avenue Unit 4, San Diego, 92105. Det. Rutledge came to my apartment for the debriefing. I gave him the details of the transaction and stated that I would arrange for another buy next week.

After the debriefing, Det. Rutledge departed, and I disconnected the decoder and removed it from the apartment. I returned to my office, and researched

William Barton in our computer database. I found a Basic-only cable subscriber by that name, who resides at the Copperfield address. The social security number listed on the customer's account is 111-66-2134. The telephone number is 280-1195. Date of installation was 9/15/95. The modified decoder was logged into the Metro Cablevision evidence locker.

On March 4th, 1997, at approximately 1125 hours (11:25 AM), the suspect approached my vehicle, which was parked in the parking lot on the south-west corner of 51st and El Cajon Blvd., behind the automobile smog repair shop. As the suspect approached, I noticed that he was not carrying any packages with him. I turned on my tape recorder, which was positioned under the passenger seat. A wireless microphone was mounted in the rear of the vehicle inside a compartment next to the wheel well. The suspect stated that he was parked about a block away on 50th and El Cajon Blvd., because he was waiting for a friend. He asked me if I was alone, and I said yes. Then, he stated that he had had a strange experience the night before with some of his pager numbers being disconnected. He said that he thought the authorities were "on to him," but later discovered that the paging company was doing some sort of account audit. I told him that he was starting to make me nervous, and he assured me that there was nothing to worry about. He then stated that he was going to get his car, so that we could complete the transaction.

While he was gone, I opened the rear doors of my van. He returned and opened the trunk of his car. I asked him if he had the two-piece descrambler unit that he had mentioned, and he said that he did. He opened a brown paper bag, and produced a cardboard box containing a CATV converter. He then showed me another smaller unit, which he referred to as a "black box." The suspect stated that he purchases these units from different companies by mail order in lots of ten (10) each. He said that the two-piece system does not have the same quality as the Pioneer decoders, but he has them just in case he runs out of Pioneer boxes. The suspect then showed me a case containing five (5) Pioneer boxes, which he was planning to sell to me. He told me that, if I wanted, I could test the boxes on the cable system in my apartment to ensure that they all worked. I told him that would not be necessary, because I trusted him. I noticed several other cable boxes in the trunk of the car, which were separately packaged.

He then told me that I should pay him now, and he closed the trunk of his vehicle. I began to count out the money, then stopped, and told him that I would rather count it out in the back of my van. He agreed. After counting out $1000.00, and handing it to him, we went back to his vehicle. He opened the trunk and handed me the case of five (5) decoders. I placed the case of decoders in the back of my van and covered it with a sheet. I asked him if it would be possible for me to meet the technician that modified the cable boxes. He indicated that the technician, whom he referred to as "Jerry," was the friend who was supposed to have met him today, but he did not show.

At that point, I removed my cap, which

was the signal to SDPD that the transaction was completed. We continued to talk until the SDPD officers approached, identified themselves, and ordered us to place our hands on top of the van. We were cuffed, frisked, and placed into a radio car. While inside, the suspect turned to me and asked if I had anything to do with this. I looked him in the eye and replied, "Do I look like I had anything to do with this?"

There was no significant exchange of conversation during this period. At one point I asked him if he thought "Jerry" may have had something to do with this, and he said, "No way."

After the officers completed their search of the vehicles, I was moved to another radio car. The suspect was taken to the substation, and I was released. Det. Rutledge informed me of the next steps that would be taken. He indicated that he would meet me at my office to test and verify that the cable boxes were modified.

Det. Rutledge brought a total of eight (8) Pioneer decoders, one (1) converter-descrambler unit, and three (3) Zenith decoders. I informed Det. Rutledge that the Zenith decoders were the type used by Southwestern Cable and could only be verified as modified on their cable system. The eight (8) Pioneer decoders and the converter-descrambler unit were all tested and verified as actively capable of unscrambling all Premium and Pay-Per-View services on Metro Cablevision cable TV system. I retrieved the first decoder, purchased from the suspect on 2/25,97, which was being stored in the Metro Cablevision evidence locker. I gave this decoder to Det. Rutledge to be included with the rest of the impounded evidence. I was instructed that a search warrant was pending and would be executed within the next few hours.

On April 25, 1997, the following letter was written and submitted to the District Attorney's office:

>D. J. Makowski
>District Attorney's Office
>330 W. Broadway, Suite 870
>San Diego, CA 92101

>Mr. Makowski.

As per our understanding, I have enclosed additional case information, which is related to the William Barton Case, #CD127445 (D.A. No. P9273701). The Case Narratives and photographs represent follow-up investigations conducted on suspects, whose names and/or telephones numbers were listed on documents recovered from Barton's apartment during the execution of a legal search warrant. These persons were identified on a list that was marked Customers.

The recovered evidence offers further proof that the devices came from the same source, which Barton indicated was his supplier. The individual, who altered the cable boxes, affixed the initials "R.L.J." to the bottom of the devices in the place where the manufacturer's serial numbers had been. According to Barton, this was done to identify his work for "warranty purposes." These initials are consistent with the markings found on the devices that Barton sold to me during the undercover sting. The initials also appeared on the boxes that were recovered from Barton's apartment during the search warrant.

All the suspects in the cases that I have enclosed, to one degree or another, identified a person vaguely fitting the description of Barton, as the man who sold them their equipment. Three of those individuals stated that they called a telephone number which they had found in a newspaper ad promoting the sale of cable television boxes. One suspect stated that he got the number from a flyer that was left on his car. Again, this is consistent with the MO that Barton used to gain access to potential customers.

I have no doubt that these individuals purchased their illegal cable equipment from Barton. The boxes are presently being stored in the Metro Cablevision Evidence locker.

If you have any questions or require the recovered evidence from these cases, please contact me at 266-5555. Thank you.

Michael Smith
Investigator

CHAPTER NINE
"R.L.J."

On March 4, 1997, during an undercover sting operation, suspect William Barton (SDPD case# 97-014242) confessed that one *James Roland* was the person he bought the cable boxes from. This information was validated by documents recovered from Barton's apartment during the execution of a search warrant. The name and address data were later confirmed by police research.

On March 6, 1997, SDPD Det. Lance Banner conducted research on the address, 1928 Middleton Drive, San Diego 92105, which was listed in Barton's documents as the residence of his illegal cable box connection. Det. Banner's data search revealed that James L. Roland was residing at 1928 Middleton Drive, San Diego 92105.

Smith initiated surveillance on the residence on April 2, 1997, and conducted periodic spot checks over the next several months. The climax came with a surprising twist as revealed in Smith's case narrative:

> On August 14th, 1997, at approximately 1045 hours (10:45 AM) I initiated surveillance of the residence located at 1928 Middleton Drive, San Diego 92105. I initially drove past the address and noted that there were two vehicles parked in the driveway, and one vehicle parked on the street in front of the residence. I made a U-turn, parked my Company vehicle about a half of a block away, and began my activity log. Because of the curvature of the street, I could not see the residence.
>
> At approximately 1055 hours (10:55), I proceeded to drive back toward the address. As I cleared the curve, and was able to see the house, I noticed that another vehicle was parked out front. This vehicle, which had not been there previously, was now parked across the driveway. It appeared to be a late model, 2-door sports car, possibly a Toyota or Nissan, red in color. Before I was able to verify the exact make and model of the vehicle, and get the

license plate number, an African American male, about 6' tall, 190 lbs., medium build, between the age of 21 -28 years-old, exited the front door of the residence, and walked down the stairs toward the street. I saw that he was carrying a white plastic bag, which appeared to contain two (2) distinctively rigid objects. The visible imprinted shape and configuration of the objects in the bag matched that of two (2) Pioneer decoders. The subject carefully watched me as I passed. I turned my eyes away, so as not to arouse suspicion. I stopped my vehicle at the corner and waited for about half a minute. Through my rear-view mirror, I observed him place the bag under the false floor in the trunk of his car. I continued across the intersection and parked. I had a clear and unobstructed view of the subject, his vehicle, and the suspect's residence. The subject got into his car and made a U-turn in the middle of the street. He then turned onto Gateway Drive and headed toward Home Avenue. I did not pursue the vehicle, but instead, decided to make door contact with the resident at 1928 Middleton Drive.

I called the San Diego Police Department's non-emergency number and asked to have an officer respond to preserve the peace, while I conducted my investigation. The three (3) officers who responded were Scott Barnett ID# 5101, Shane Lancer ID# 5276 and Donna Gentry ID# 5337. I briefed the officers on the case, the Penal Code section, and the procedures that I would follow.

At approximately 1225 hours (12:25 PM), I approached the residence and made door contact. A man, who later identified himself as James L. Roland, got up from the sofa and answered the door. The front door was open, and the television, VCR and cable box were in clear view through the iron mesh screen. I asked the man if his name was James Roland and he said "Yes." I identified myself as an Investigator for Metro Cablevision and presented him with my photo identification. I told him that I wished to speak with him about the cable box that he had on top of the television and requested permission to enter the residence. Roland stated that we could not enter the house without a search warrant and proceeded to close the front door. I told him that I had already seen the decoder on the television, and Roland stated, "I'll give you the box, but you can't come in without a search warrant." He then slammed the door shut.

Ofc. Barnett immediately initiated the process for a telephonic search warrant. About five minutes later, the owner of the house, Martha Lopez, drove up and parked in front of the house. She got out of the vehicle and asked Ofc. Barnett what was going on. Ofc. Barnett explained the situation and asked if she was the owner of the house. She said that she was. He asked if she would allow us to enter the residence to continue our investigation, and she granted us permission to enter.

Upon entering the residence, I observed two (2) Pioneer decoders on a chair in the kitchen area. One of these boxes was warm to the touch, indicating that it had recently been connected to an AC power source. The other box was not warm. I inspected these devices and found that they had been tampered with. Roland stated that we could take the boxes. I asked where the rest of the boxes were, and he said that there were no other boxes. When I said that I did not believe him, he became hostile, and shouted, "Fuck you!" Ofc. Barnett proceeded to diffuse the situation, by subduing the suspect and placing him in handcuffs.

The owner of the house, Ms. Lopez, had given us permission to search the entire house, inside and out. Upon inspection of the bathroom, I found, sitting in the tub, two (2) cardboard cartons containing ten (10) Pioneer decoders each. These cartons were imprinted with the Pioneer logo, the PIONEER name, and BA-6310A CATV CONVERTER information on the outside. This is the same type of carton that is used by Metro Cablevision to transport decoders from one location to another. The decoders inside these cartons were still wrapped in plastic in the exact same fashion as used by Cablevision Materiel personnel. Attached to each plastic wrapping was a small paper sticker with a date stamped on it. These date identification stickers were the same as those used by Cablevision

Materiel personnel to identify the trucked-out expiration date of CATV decoders. The serial numbers were still attached to the devices, and none of this equipment had been opened or modified. The serial numbers were researched by Cablevision Materiel personnel and found to be the property of Metro Cablevision. This equipment was unreported stolen. Roland voluntarily stated, without being asked, that all the cable boxes and related cable equipment belonged to him, and that no one else in the house had anything to do with it.

Further inspection of the residence revealed ten (10) more Pioneer decoders in a cardboard carton, which was the same as used by Metro Cablevision to transport equipment from one location to another. The decoders in this carton had been tampered with, and apparently were modified. Most of the serial numbers had been removed, and the initials "R.L.J." were marked on the bottom of nine (9) of those boxes. The same initials were found on boxes sold by William Barton (SDPD Case# 97-014242).

The inspection uncovered three (3) more Pioneer boxes, one (1) Scientific Atlanta box, six (6) Zenith decoders (which are the type used by Southwestern Cable TV), computer chips, a chip activator (cube), pirate box modification tools, equipment, and materials.

All the cable boxes and modification-related articles were photographed, seized as evidence, removed, and released to Metro Cablevision and are now being stored in the Security Evidence Locker. Roland was arrested and taken into custody. We departed the area at approximately 1425 hours (2:25 PM)

The unreported stolen cable boxes had come directly from the company's warehouse. Smith was anxious for the District Attorney to take the case and unravel the mystery of the missing decoders, but. . . that never happened. Roland was found guilty of felony cable theft, but never served jail time. The prosecuting attorney downgraded the charges to possession of a single cable box. Roland was released without revealing the identity of his cable box supplier inside the company.

"Sometimes we put just a little too much faith in the *system*," thought Smith, as he filed away Roland's case.

There was nothing more that could be done. The defendant was ordered to pay restitution to the company, given a substantial fine, and ordered to perform 40 hours of community service work. His Fourth Amendment Right was abridged for three years during his probation. He was ordered to cease and desist the manufacturing and modification of all cable television equipment.

Smith sighed.

CHAPTER TEN
"A Single Grain of Sand"

Dorothy Rader was a real piece of work. In all the years working with law enforcement, conducting scores of investigations and sting operations, and arresting countless suspects, Smith had never encountered a case like this. Not only was the suspect guilty of stealing cable television service, but she lied about it to her attorney. Seeing an opportunity for a huge payday, Farrokh Bashir, her defense attorney, manipulated the pre-trial prosecutor into believing that Smith falsified his report just to score another arrest. Bashir persuaded the deputy DA to toss the case out for *lack of evidence.* The attorney was hungrily eyeing "deep pockets" and conspired to build a case against the company by attacking Smith's credibility and integrity. Bashir knew he could convince a jury that his clients' arrest was based upon false testimony and manufactured evidence. He promised to prove that Smith was untrained, incompetent, and unfit for the job.

Smith opened the file and reviewed his testimony.

> On Tuesday January 23, 2007, I received a call on my cell phone from field service technician, Jorge Montego. He told me he was at an address in Vista doing some construction rebuild work. He said the residents at that address were stealing cable TV services and that I should go and investigate what was going on. He indicated there was only one customer in the building which was a triplex. He said the other two units were tapped into the customer's line on the roof. He said the customer in Unit C had informed him that the residents in Unit A and Unit B tapped into her line when she went to work.
>
> I asked Montego to meet me back at my office. (I was in the field at the time he called.) Later that morning Montego came to my office. We discussed the situation further. He indicated that he was doing a construction rebuild at 657 Cypress Avenue in Vista, and had been approached by the customer in Unit C. The customer

told him that the residents in Unit A and Unit B were tapping into her line. This occurred when she had gone to work. I believe Montego may have drawn a rough sketch of the building layout, indicating the locations of each of the units. He stated that Unit C was the upstairs apartment.

Montego said he had observed the cable connections on the roof and asked the customer if she knew her line was being tapped into. The customer then indicated that the residents in Unit A and Unit B were tapping into the line when she went to work. Montego did not disconnect the wires, because he wanted me to see how they were spliced together. He stated that he was concerned the two non-customers would splice into the paying customer's line again. He said that he did not want to waste the time and effort required to install new wires from the telephone pole, just to have the customer's line spliced into again. He indicated that the job was a two-pole back yard service installation, and he would have to run three separate drops for each of the three units.

Montego provided the details of what

he had observed, and a Violation Report was written. The report states, "Customer in Unit C stated that residents in Unit A and B were splicing into her cable when she went to work." Montego confirmed the statement was accurate.

Early afternoon, I went to the residence at 657 Cypress Avenue in Vista. As I approached the address, I observed that the building was at the end of an easement and was a split-level design. I looked for any signs of tampering that may have been visible from the ground in front of the residence. I only observed some wires coming from the roof down the front of the building. One wire was going to Unit A and the other wire was going to Unit B. The wires appeared to be old. I also observed two newly installed cable wires attached to the building and going to Unit A. These cable wires appeared to have been installed by a professional technician. I visually traced the wires from the front of the unit around the side and toward the back. There was a splitter attached to the building that was feeding the two lines from a single line going further back than I could see.

I knocked on the door of Unit A. A woman who identified herself as Dorothy Rader answered the door. I identified myself as an employee for Metro Cablevision and presented her with my photo identification. I explained that I had received a report that there were some wires on the roof that probably should not be there, and that I was conducting a follow-up inspection. I indicated that the wires were illegally connected to another unit. Rader stated that she had called Metro for service and thought I was there to connect the service for her. I explained that I was not a service technician, and that I was there to inspect the wires on the roof. She told me that was okay and that the wires on the roof were a mess.

I then asked Rader who had installed the new cable wires on the outside of her unit. She stated that the Metro technician had installed the wires. I asked if I could continue my inspection by entering the back yard to visually trace the wires. She indicated that would be okay. I went to the gate on the side of the unit and attempted to open it. It appeared to be locked from the inside. I immediately went back to the door, knocked again and Rader answered. I told her the gate appeared to be locked from the inside. She said she would have her daughter open the gate. A few minutes later the gate opened, and I observed a teenage female standing inside the gate. She turned and walked back toward the back yard, turned the corner, and went into the residence through the back door.

I continued my inspection of the cable wires attached to the side of the unit. I saw that the two wires were fed from a splitter connected to a single cable wire. The single cable wire was attached to the side of the house and continued to the rear of the unit. I observed that this wire was not connected to anything and was simply hanging from the eve of the building. I then walked back toward the gate. There was a ladder resting on the side of the building which reached the roof. I climbed the ladder and walked along the roof toward the split upper level. I observed a mass of cable wires which were connected by a series of splitters. All the wires and splitters were attached to a single cable wire that fed service to the building. It appeared as if the wires had been in that condition for many years. The wires were old.

I climbed back down the ladder and approached the front door. I knocked on the door again, and again Rader answered. I told her I had been on the roof and saw the mess of wires. I said that I was going to disconnect the wires and remove them. Rader indicated that the wires had been that way before she lived there, and that they had never worked anyway. I went to my vehicle and put on my tool belt. I went back through the gate and climbed the ladder to the roof. I cut out the splitters and the non-subscriber cable wires. I reattached the cable lines properly for the customer in Unit C. I gathered the cable wires and splitters, climbed back down the ladder, and returned to my vehicle. I put the wires into a plastic bag to be discarded later. I took off my tool belt and placed it back inside my vehicle. I then approached Unit B and attempted to make contact. No one was home. I believe I may have left a door hanger on the door, but I cannot recall specifically. I got back into my vehicle and left the residence.

Later that week I contacted Montego and informed him that I had contacted the resident in Unit A. I told him I believed it was okay to finish the construction rebuild.

On Friday February 9, 2007, I conducted a series of follow-up inspections on several open cases in Oceanside and Vista. Prior to making the physical inspections I checked the account status of each address in ICOMS the Metro Cablevision customer database. I verified there had been no change in status on the accounts associated with the open cable theft investigations. I inspected eleven locations before arriving at 657 Cypress Avenue.

As I approached the residence, I observed a gentleman outside near the garage area. I am not certain what he was doing, but as I approached, I asked him if he was the resident in Unit B. I do not remember what his exact response was, but the indication was that he did not reside in Unit B but did reside in Unit A. He told me that someone was home in Unit A. I was wearing my Metro ID badge which was visible on my uniform. I did not tell him why I was there and proceeded to the door of Unit A. I do not remember if the door was open, but I knocked, and a woman answered. She identified herself as Rader's sister. I asked her if she was a resident there, and I believe she stated that she was visiting. I explained that I was from Metro Cablevision, and I showed her my ID badge. I told her I was conducting a follow-up inspection and wanted to look at the cable wires on the roof. I asked for permission to go into the backyard and permission was granted.

The reason I went to Unit A was because the ladder to the roof was in their backyard, and I needed to climb the ladder to see if Unit C was still connected correctly. By this time, and according to ICOMS, the construction rebuilds had been complete, and three new cable drops had been installed from the telephone pole to the house. The wires were neatly tucked inside a vertical conduit from the upper split-level roof to the lower roof eve. The three wires appeared to be attached under the eve. There was no indication of tampering at that location.

I observed a piece of cable resting on the awning in the backyard of Unit A, which had not been there during my previous visit. I climbed back down the ladder and walked to the back of the unit. That is when I observed the illegal connection. The unauthorized wire was connected to the single house wire that fed the splitter installed by the Metro technician on January 9, 2007, in the initial house wiring preparation. The white wire was a non-Metro cable and appeared to be an old VCR coaxial cable. This wire was then connected to another length of cable that was draped over the fence and into the yard next door. I was able to observe that the wire was connected to a splitter under the eve. The splitter was attached to the active cable line for Unit C. Upon discovering the illegal connection, I immediately left the premises. I did not take photographs of the connection and did not approach anyone with regards to the illegal connection. I conducted one more follow-up inspection at another address, and then returned to my office to update my case files and database. I prepared my Field Investigation documents with the intention of contacting the residents in Unit A the next morning, Saturday February 10, 2009. The documents included the Field Investigator's Case Log, Field Report, Questionnaire, copy of PC593d, Violation Report and screen shots from ICOMS (including Customer Maintenance, Work Order, previous customer - Customer Maintenance, Unit B Customer Maintenance, and Unit C Customer Maintenance).

On Saturday February 10, 2007, I drove to a location near the address at 657 Cypress Avenue. It was approximately 9:15 AM. I placed a call to the Sheriff's Dispatch non-emergency line at approximately 9:20 AM. I identified myself to the Dispatcher, stating that I was an investigator employed by Mero Cablevision, and that I was in the process of investigating some folks which we suspected using the cable television service without paying for it. And, that I would like to have a deputy to respond, and standby to preserve the peace while I conduct the investigation. I gave the Dispatcher my personal information, my cell phone number, the location of the residence and the location where I wanted to meet the deputy.

Approximately 10 minutes later two deputies arrived in separate patrol cars. The deputies were N. Cochran ID#0602, and B. Masterson ID#2830. When the deputies arrived, I proceeded to explain the facts and circumstances that I had observed. I told the deputies that the case involved a violation of California Penal Code 593d, cable theft. I stated the procedures I would follow, and if consent was granted to enter the residence, proceed to gather additional facts and evidence. And, if the elements of the crime were present, I might also make a citizen's arrest. If so, it would be a cite and release.

Around this initial meeting and briefing, Deputy Cochran's recollection of the facts differ from my own. He recalls having me sign a Citizen's Arrest form before going to the door to make contact. I do not recall signing the form beforehand since the document would only be valid if an arrest were to occur. And, I had not gathered enough facts and evidence to make an arrest. Deputy Cochran also recalled that I showed him photographs of the illegal connections before we contacted the residents. That was not possible since I had not taken any photographs at that point. I surmised that Deputy Cochran may have recalled a memory of a subsequent investigation to which he responded a few months later a preserve the peace, and at which time I did show him photographs.

After the briefing Deputy Cochran advised caution in approaching this residence. He was not specific as the reason why we should exercise caution or the nature of his suspicions. But upon his recommendation, we proceeded with caution.

We arrived at the location and parked our vehicles a short distance away from the suspects' residence. We walked to the door. I may have knocked on the door and then stepped back, or Deputy Cochran may have knocked on door. I do not recall specifically which of us knocked on the door. A few minutes later a man who identified himself as Matthew Patterson answered the door. Deputy Cochran asked him if he was resident there and he indicated that he was. Patterson asked what was going on and as I recall, the deputy asked if he would not mind stepping outside. Once the doorway was clear and the deputy felt the situation was secured, he deferred Patterson's questions to me. I stepped forward and identified myself as an investigator for Metro Cablevision, showed him my photo identification and told him that I would like to speak to him about the cable TV connections inside his residence. I asked if it would be okay to come inside and inspect the televisions and cable connections inside the residence. He said that would be okay and granted us permission to enter the residence. Patterson turned and entered the residence first. Prior to entering I advised Patterson that the deputies were present as a precaution for safety and to preserve the peace, and that this investigation was being conducted for Metro Cablevision. He indicated that he understood, and I, and the two deputies entered the residence.

Upon entering I observed an entertainment center near the front door. There was a 19" color television sitting inside the unit. The television was not turned on. I indicated to one of the deputies (I cannot remember which one) that I wanted to check to see if the wire had been disconnected in the backyard. I proceeded to check outside and verified that the line was still connected in the fashion that I had observed the day before. I returned to the living room.

I asked for permission to turn the television on and to view the channels it was receiving. Patterson granted me permission to turn on the television. The channel it was tuned to initially was Channel 10-KGTV. I clicked through the channels and saw that the television was receiving all the basic and expanded basic programming. I used my digital camera and took photos of the entertainment center and the television.

I asked Patterson who had connected the cable, and he stated, "I don't know."

"How long has the cable been

connected to the television?" I asked.

"I have no idea," he responded.

"Did you know the service was connected illegally?"

"No, I didn't. But if it is connected illegally, I have an idea who did it."

"Who is that?" I asked.

"A kid that spends time here a lot," he said.

"What's his name?"

"Robert."

"So, you believe Robert is the person that illegally connected the cable?"

"Yes."

During this time both deputies were present in the room with Patterson and me. Yet, I was not aware of what the deputies were doing or where they were standing, as my focus was on the television and verifying the connection to the Metro cable service. Patterson, however, was seated on the couch.

I asked Patterson if there was anyone else in the house besides himself, and he stated that his girlfriend was in the bedroom. I then asked Patterson if there were any other televisions in the house and he indicated that there was a TV in the bedroom. I asked for permission to inspect the television in the bedroom, and he granted permission.

Deputy Masterson entered the bedroom first. I waited outside until I was instructed that it was okay to enter. Upon entering I observed a 57" color television facing the bed. The television was on and was tuned to Channel 35-Discovery Channel. Dorothy Rader was sitting on the bed. I do not recall what she was wearing as my attention was focused on the television. I clicked through the channels and verified that the television was connected to the Metro cable service. It was receiving all the basic and expanded basic programming. I took photographs of the television, and then turned my attention to Rader.

I asked her if she remembered when I came to her house a few weeks prior to disconnecting the cable on the roof.

"No," she replied. "There have been so many Metro technicians here that I can't remember."

"Can you tell me how the cable service got hooked up?"

"I don't know," she said. "I guess Metro hooked it up."

"I know Metro didn't hook up the cable. Tell me how it got connected."

"Someone hooked it up."

"What is his name?" I asked.

"I don't want to say," Rader replied.

"I believe it was Robert, the young man who spends time here. Did Robert connect the cable service for you?"

"Yes, he connected it."

"Why would he do that?" I asked.

"I asked him to."

"When did he connect the service?"

"It was Super Bowl Sunday."

"What did you tell Mr. Patterson about the cable?"

"What do you mean?"

"What did you tell him about how the cable service got connected?"

"I told him that I had Robert hook it up for me."

"So, he knew it was connected illegally?"

"Well, yeah."

"And did he know it was connected on Super Bowl Sunday?"

"Yes."

"And what was his response?"

"Matt said it has to be unhooked by the end of the game, but it never got unhooked."

During this time while I was interviewing Rader, Deputy Masterson was standing near the door. I do not know her exact position, as I was focused on the interview. I walked out of the bedroom and back into the living room. As I recall Patterson was already handcuffed, and still sitting on the couch.

I asked Patterson, "Do you know when the cable got hooked up?"

He responded, "No."

"Are you sure?" I inquired.

"I'm sure."

I looked at my notes and then said, "According to Ms. Rader, she told you that Robert hooked up the cable on Super Bowl Sunday. Do you remember that conversation with her?"

"Well," he replied, "yes, I guess she did tell me."

"And do you remember telling her that the cable had to be disconnected by the end of the game?"

He admitted telling Rader before he left town that she needed to have the cable disconnected right after the Super Bowl.

"So, then you knew the cable had been connected illegally, is that right?"

"Yes, I did. I will take responsibility. Arrest me. I don't have anything else to say."

With the facts and evidence that had been presented to me along with their admissions, I believed there was enough probable cause to place both Patterson and Rader under citizen's arrest for violations of California Penal Code 593d(a)(1). I expected that Deputy Cochran would write citations for them and release them on the spot, but instead, he took them both into custody. Deputy Masterson accompanied Rader into the bedroom where she changed clothes, then handcuffed her and escorted her out of the room. Deputy Cochran transported both arrestees to the Vista Sheriff's station.

Deputy Masterson stayed behind while I photographed and then disconnected the illegal cable connections. There were three teenagers present, and they were engaged in conversation with Deputy Masterson. I did not listen to their conversation and did not know what they spoke about. I removed the connections, and we departed the area at approximately 10:25 AM.

I returned to my office in Oceanside, and immediately began typing my report. Upon completing my report, I took a copy to the Sheriff's substation in Vista along with a CD containing the photographs I had taken at the scene of the crime.

Smith reviewed the photos.

During the trial Smith used several exhibits to explain the circumstances of his investigation. He methodically explained how the connections had been made, and the way Rader and Patterson were using the cable without authorization. His presentation was professional and precise. Despite his best effort all the jurors were not convinced of his innocence.

Smith was represented by two highly experienced corporate attorneys, Steven Pollachi and Rita Delano. They had been hired by Metro's corporate legal department to defend Smith. Even their polished words and arguments did not convince all the jurors.

Smith realized his future lay in the hands of twelve strangers. Twelve people whom he had never met, who knew nothing of his background or his accomplishments, would decide his fate. The words spoken by Judge Caufield at the start of the trial echoed in his mind.

"This is a civil trial to determine if Metro Cablevision employee, Michael Devon Smith, acted inappropriately in his investigation and arrest of plaintiffs, Dorothy Rader, and Matthew Patterson, that he is accused of falsifying a report.

"In a criminal trial the defendant must be found guilty beyond a reasonable doubt. However, in a civil trial the defendant is found guilty by a preponderance of the evidence. Whereas there must be considerable evidence to reach a conviction in a criminal trial, the scales of justice in a civil trial can be determined by *a single grain of sand*."

EPILOGUE

Smith opened an email that had been sent from the corporate office. It contained a FAX document submitted to his attorney by a news outlet. He read the FAX.

To: Steven M. Pollachi
Company: Lords Warfield & Pollachi LLP
Dear Attorney:

We have noted the above-mentioned case with interest and would like to include it in a forthcoming issue of the weekly Daily Journal "Verdicts & Settlements" section. The Los Angeles Daily Journal (established 1888) and the San Francisco Daily Journal (established 1893) are the country's leading daily legal newspapers and the premier publications for court cases, profiles of judges and neutrals and for regular coverage of dozens of practice areas.

Below/attached please find a formatted version by way of a rough draft of the case for your review. If there are material errors in the below/attached report, or if you have additional information, please respond within three (3) business days by FAX ... EMAIL or the attached will be printed as it currently appears. Feel free to mark up the page(s) submitted herewith or send additional pages.

Please confirm receipt of this notice by faxing back the report with your initials. If there are any inaccuracies in the attached report, please fax or email us those changes. The Daily Journal Corporation reserves the right to exercise editorial prerogative regarding any submitted case reports.

We look forward to hearing from you. In the future, please consider submitting any cases that you would like us to include in the Daily Journal "Verdicts & Settlements" section either by visiting our web site (www.dailyjoumal.com) or by fax to (213) 229-5403 to the attention of Tess Santiago. Thank you very much.

Sincerely.

Thomas Henry, Esq.
Editor, Verdicts & Settlements
Tel (213) 229-5555
Fax (213) 228-5555
verdicts@dailyjournal.com
www.dailyjournal.com

RESULT DATE: April 28, 2009
Dorothy Rader, Matthew Patterson v. Metro Cablevision, Michael Smith (37-2007-00054790-CU-NP-NC)
Hon. Jason B. Caufield
San Diego Superior
TOPIC: Civil Rights
SUB-TOPIC: False Imprisonment
FURTHER DESCRIPTION: Negligent Training
VERDICT: $12,806

ATTORNEY:
Plaintiff – Farrokh Bashir (Bashir Law Group, Vista).
Defendant - Steven M. Pollachi, Rita H. Delano (Lords, Warfield & Pollachi, LLP, Poway).

TECHNICAL:
Plaintiff – Mark Minos, police practices and procedures, San Diego.
Defendant - Collin Jones, police practices and procedures, Fallbrook

FACTS:
Metro Cablevision (Metro) investigator, Michael Smith, disconnected an unlawful cable connection that he discovered connected to plaintiffs Matthew Patterson and Dorothy Rader's Vista apartment. Several weeks later,

he discovered a new illegal connection was in place.

On Feb. 10, 2006, in the presence of two police officers, Smith interviewed the plaintiffs about their knowledge of the illegal connection. They admitted that they were aware of the connection. Smith placed them under citizen's arrest, and they were taken into custody. Ultimately, the prosecutor dropped the charges against them

The plaintiffs then sued Metro and Smith for false arrest, false imprisonment, and negligence.

PLAINTIFF'S CONTENTIONS:
The plaintiffs claimed that they were attempting to purchase cable and were unaware that the service had been unlawfully connected. They alleged that Smith did not thoroughly investigate the theft because he failed to speak with any other neighbors. The plaintiffs also claimed that Metro was negligent in its hiring and supervision of Smith.

DEFENDANTS CONTENTIONS:
Metro claimed that the plaintiffs had admitted to committing a crime and therefore the arrest was perfectly lawful. It claimed that

the plaintiffs admitted their knowledge of the illegal connection prior to the 2007 Super Bowl and acknowledged that one of their children's friends had connected it illegally. It further argued that the plaintiffs suffered no actual injuries because of the arrest.

DAMAGES:
The plaintiffs sought damages for emotional distress, caused by being arrested in front of their children, and $40,000 in attorney fees. They did not claim, however, to have needed medical or psychiatric care.

JURY TRIAL:
Length. six days.
Poll, 12-0 (no negligence),
11-1 (against Rader's false arrest claim),
10-2 (against Patterson's false arrest claim).
Deliberation, 1.75 hours

SETTLEMENT DISCUSSIONS: The plaintiffs demanded $5,900 each; the defendants offered $7,000 via C.C.P. Section 998.

RESULT: At the close of the plaintiffs' evidence, the court ordered a verdict to be directed in favor of Metro on the issue of negligence. The jury found in favor of Smith. The court awarded the defense $12,806 in costs.

OTHER INFORMATION:
During trial, the court refused to admit evidence that the charges were dropped holding that whether the prosecutor chose to pursue the case was irrelevant as to whether the citizen's arrest was lawful. The court also excluded the officer's opinion testimony stating that the citizen's arrest was properly performed, that there was independent probable cause for the arrest, and that the arrest was properly and professionally performed.

After two years of painstaking interrogatories, interviews, depositions, and pre-trial preparation, it was finally over. Smith had barely escaped a catastrophe. He breathed a heavy sigh of relief as he closed the Rader file.

"This case is one for the books," he mused.

A moment later, the telephone rang. Smith picked up the receiver, placed it close to his ear, and spoke.

"Hello. Metro Cablevision, Michael Smith speaking. How can I help you?"

BOOKS BY THIS AUTHOR

The Bell - Circles Of Awareness

The Bell: Unveiling the Subliminal Realm

The Bell embarks on a profound journey into the depths of metaphysics, brain evolution, and quantum mechanics, weaving a tapestry of ideas that challenge our understanding of reality and consciousness. This narrative is the first step in a seven-tier quest to uncover the hidden subconscious alter ego and awaken the dormant god-consciousness within each of us.

Metaphysics and the Nature of Reality

At its core, The Bell delves into metaphysics, the branch of philosophy that explores the fundamental nature of reality, existence, and the universe. It probes beyond the physical world to understand the underlying principles governing everything. By examining the metaphysical aspects of existence, *The Bell* invites readers to question the nature of reality and consider the deeper connections that bind the universe together.

Delusions Of Grandeur - A Schizophrenic Reality

.This book sheds light on the challenges faced by high-functioning individuals with schizophrenia. Many of these individuals are successful professionals in positions of power and authority such as businessmen and women, educators, and politicians. They often conceal their condition due to the fear of stigma affecting their relationships, job opportunities, and public image. Despite this, it is crucial for them to overcome their fear and guilt to pursue their dreams and aspirations. The book also explores the idea of schizophrenia as a manifestation of innate psychic phenomena. The author's personal journey from youth to adulthood is recounted, highlighting various disappointments and personal failures that led to mental depression. Through meditation and self-hypnosis, the author achieved a higher level of consciousness and unlocked his "god consciousness" hidden in his inner subconscious mind.

Ghosts Of Piracy Past - Cable Theft Investigations

With the expansion of cable television services in the 1990's the public's hunger for video entertainment grew proportionately. Unfortunately, cable piracy and theft of services became rampant, resulting in millions of dollars in lost revenue. The overwhelming criminal activity forced cable companies to hire specially trained investigators to mitigate losses by actively pursuing the arrest and prosecution of cable pirates. California Penal Code 593d gave cable companies the tools to pursue active criminal investigations. Law enforcement agencies, including DHS, IRS, FBI, Secret Service, and local Police and Sheriff's departments, worked closely with private sector investigators to stop the spread of intellectual property theft.

Little Sadiq - The Door Of No Return

In 16th-century Africa, a young Mandinka boy sets out on a perilous journey through rugged jungle terrain to a distant village. Facing mortal danger, he completes the journey and reaches his destination. There, he recounts his journey to the village elders. Later, he meets a witch doctor, who places him in a deep hypnotic trance and implants subliminal messages in his mind. When Sadiq sets out for home, his world is turned upside down.

Sadiq begins an adventure that is magical and legendary.

Little Sadiq - Visions

Little Sadiq has gone home with the other boys, and Shango has gone alone. There are concerns about Sadiq's sanity as he continues to commune with Abdul, the ghost boy.
VISIONS reveals the hidden truths about the war between the Mandingos and the Fulani and how Europeans were able to capitalize on that division. Mande and Fula's rivalry threatened the fabric of African society and resulted in millions of sub-Saharan Africans dying or being sold into slavery.

Our story begins with Sadiq's realization that he may have inadvertently caused the destruction of the ancestral village! We find him amid a crisis as enemy raiders have located his village and are preparing for an assault. Backed by Portuguese slavers and armed with European muskets, the invaders set their sights on Ndande.

ACKNOWLEDGEMENT

I would like to acknowledge and thank all my law enforcement colleagues who accompanied me on these amazing adventures. Without their support and friendship, the theft of service program would not have succeeded. I am grateful for the relationships I developed, the task forces and intelligence organizations I was a part of: H.T.C.I.A, C.A.T.C.H, A.S.I.S., and FBI InfraGard.

A special thanks to all my cable cronies with whom I interacted daily. It was never really about the job; it was about *relationships.*

ABOUT THE AUTHOR

Darno Von Dejohnette

I was born in Dermott, AR, on August 27, 1951. At age five, my family moved to Chicago, IL, where I lived until age 18. I graduated from Albert G. Lane Technical High School in 1969 and joined the United States Air Force. After being honorably discharged from the military, I traveled to California and enrolled in Compton Community College. I majored in journalism and eventually landed a job with Rockwell International Space Division as a student intern in Public Relations. Over the next several years, I worked in various fields and occupations, as a free-lance reporter, laboratory technician, factory worker, security guard, police officer, television technician, and finally, cybercrime investigator. I reside in Oceanside, California with my wife, and we have been blessed with two wonderful children.

www.ingramcontent.com/pod-product-compliance
Lightning Source LLC
Chambersburg PA
CBHW070624220526
45466CB00001B/95